AFRICA IN FASHION

LAURENCE KING

First published in Great Britain in 2022 by
Laurence King Student & Professional
An imprint of Quercus Editions Ltd
Carmelite House
50 Victoria Embankment
London EC4Y 0DZ

An Hachette UK company

A CIP catalogue record for this book is available
from the British Library

TPB ISBN 9781913947958
Ebook ISBN 9781529419856

10 9 8 7 6 5 4 3 2 1
Designed by TwoSheds Design
Cover image by Kadara Enyeasi

Printed and bound in China by C&C Offset Printing Co., Ltd.

Papers used by Quercus are from well-managed forests and
other responsible sources.

I dedicate this work
to three phenomenal ladies:
my mother Obaapanyin, Adwoa Kwakowa;
my wife, Efua Koufie;
my daughter, Ama Kwakowa Nimo.

Front cover
Mtwana neck piece in orange, brown and gold by Jiamini.
The Mtwana signature neck piece from Jiamini's
Mung'ung'uti (Spine) collection combines dexterously
beaded leather that is detailed with an 18k gold-plated
brass spine-inspired sculpture.

Photographer: Kadara Enyeasi
Model: Zainab Alade
Represented by 90s Models Management, Nigeria
Make up: Obidike Uchechukwu
Producer: A Whitespace Creative Agency
Produced with support from Ethical Fashion Initiative
and EU International partnerships

Back cover
Woven textile by Johanna Bramble.

AFRICA IN FASHION

Luxury, Craft and Textile Heritage

Ken Kweku Nimo

Foreword by Deola Sagoe

Laurence King Publishing

Chapter 3:
New Wave of African Talent 94

Foreword

〰〰〰

Africa *is always* in fashion.

This book represents a particular point along the continuum of our appreciation of what Africa means in fashion. We are woven into this continuum as Ken alludes to in the sub-chapter 'Woven Stories and Ancient Fabrics'. Yet we are also sovereign; our personal domains seek definition, perhaps even restitution, as is subtly implied in the sub-chapter 'Colonialism', ('Europe's grand imperialist venture in Africa').

Africa in Fashion is an ambitious book. Its size may not immediately signal this but in its slimness is precisely where the ambition lies – simultaneously drawing our attention to everything that is put in, as well as everything that is left out. This book does not presume to tell the entire story of Africa in fashion –what singular work would dare to state that as its mission?

What this book accomplishes is successfully pulling together a wide array of tributaries of information, into a river of knowledge, which you, dear reader, must have been thirsting for in the first place – otherwise, you wouldn't have reached out for this book upon the shelf.

When I was drawn to fashion, I was first seduced by our indigenous fabrics. It felt to me like a strange arrangement had been made among everyone else on Earth to play down, to overlook, what I could see was patently woven magic! It surprised me how taken for granted this treasure trove of resources, African textiles, was. Over the years my appreciation of this magic has never waned. So, for anyone like me, go straight to the sub-chapter 'A Textile Heritage' and read on with a smile on your face!

I am appreciative to Ken for profiling some of the heroes of modern African fashion design in the sub-chapter 'Generation Couture'. They include Shade Thomas-Fahm, with whom I have had the pleasure of collaborating, and Kofi Ansah with whom I had so many deep conversations about where to go next with design – we were unfortunately robbed of our plans to collaborate by his passing.

My brand has been synonymous with 'luxury' from the outset, partly because of my laser-like focus on the details in my designs, as well as a personal ethos that 'luxury exists in the eye of the beholder'. And I am glad that more and more cultures around the world are appreciating the African eye!

We are just at the tipping point of what Africa means in luxury – so I suggest that Ken dedicate his next project to *Africa in Luxury*.

Deola Sagoe

Introduction

〰〰〰〰〰

The universal appeal of fashion is evident in the speed by which the latest styles and trends permeate global markets. Catalysed in contemporary times by disruptive digital media, e-commerce, and integrated supply chain and distribution channels, fashion has become one of the biggest sectors of the global economy. In Africa, the fashion and textile industry is underpinned by a production value chain capable of fostering economic growth and job creation in the context of a bulging youth population, while mitigating the threats posed by fast fashion.

Until the late twentieth century, Africa was confined to the periphery of the global fashion economy, benefiting marginally as the source of raw material and as the terminal market for finished goods. Africa's post-independence efforts at leveraging indigenous textile and apparel industries for economic growth have been slow to bear fruit. Yet, despite the endemic challenges, African fashion has thrived. Propelled by vibrant indigenous production and distribution networks, it has weathered decades of subjugation and exploitation to produce some of the world's greatest designers. Indeed, the twenty-first century has witnessed a surge in Africa's creative economy as a generation of designers adopt cutting-edge technology to harness the potential of indigenous production techniques, media and handcrafting skills. Africa's rich cultural and craft heritage, together with its abundance of natural and human resources and relative socio-economic stability in recent times, can foster an indigenous industry for the manufacture of high-value and craft-oriented luxury goods.

This volume is divided into three chapters. In Chapter 1, we explore the history of the development of African fashion under the vectors of trade, culture, colonialism and globalization. We focus, subsequently, on its rich heritage in textiles, accessories and embellishments.

In Chapter 2 we profile the most prolific African designers operating from or out of Africa – beginning with the generation of pioneering designers whose work has stimulated a substantive and global African fashion. We also discuss the exigencies of developing a truly sustainable fashion and luxury industry with international reach.

Finally, the last chapter gives voice to the contemporary designers shaping Africa's cultural renaissance. The opening pages are a showcase for a wide range of designers comprising menswear, womenswear and accessories such as leather goods and jewellery. This is followed by interviews with thirteen distinguished contemporary designers. Each of the curated brands, whether established or emerging, is part of the kaleidoscope of creative talent in Africa's rapidly evolving fashion industry.

Page 6
Yana design from Tropical
Galactica Surreal collection
2020 by Deola Sagoe.

Page 8
Origami triangular-pleated
puff blouse and corseted
palazzo pants from Season 3
collection 2021 by Duaba
Serwa.

Opposite
Paw Pot two-tone design by
AAKS. This popular mini
bag is crafted from woven
raffia in the brand's signature
shape. It is accented with
tasseled leather trim and
has a linen pouch.

CHAPTER 1

African Fashion History

Fashion is a social phenomenon that has captivated people throughout the world throughout history. Defined loosely, it is the distinctive sartorial style and adornment of people from diverse cultures and social classes. Beyond this, it is at once constructive and subversive, the outcome of people striving for social capital and status in almost every society with a degree of stratification. However, because of a predominant misconception of fashion as solely an agent of western modernity, the dress practices of many cultures within Africa and its diaspora, have received little attention in conventional histories of global fashion.

Today, the narrative of an 'unfashionable' Africa is well contested and gradually being replaced by a compelling counter-narrative.

This chapter starts by exploring the history of the development of African fashion under the vectors of trade, culture, colonialism and globalization. This exploration culminates with a discussion of the ways in which Africa has influenced fashion 'beyond Africa' throughout the centuries. The chapter then moves on to take a closer look at the rich heritage of the continent in sub-chapters devoted more specifically to textiles and to accessories and embellishments.

A History Retold

Recent media attention and literature on African fashion has highlighted its potency as a medium of cultural expression, with a kaleidoscope of textiles, accessories and art forms constituting a truly dynamic sartorial discourse.[1] The rich history of African fashion remains widely unacknowledged in the context of global fashion, however. Here, it is retold through the vectors of trade, culture, colonialism and globalization, and explored throughout the continent and beyond.

Trade

Before the arrival of the first European ships, inhabitants of many of Africa's ancient empires including Ghana, Mali and Songhai traded across regional and territorial boundaries. The nexus of trade in precolonial Africa was remarkably complex, with routes traversing the west, central and northern regions of Africa and across the Mediterranean to Europe. Trading centres were connected by major highways with safety patrols and toll points dotting the seemingly trackless forest and vast desert terrains.

    While the currency for trade varied across regions, ethnic groups and empires, it comprised primarily gold dust, brass, iron, copper, strips of cloth and ivory. In the ninth century, the caliphs of North Africa minted their own gold dinars to trade with merchants from Spain and other parts of Europe.

    Between the fifth and late nineteenth centuries, trade fostered the rise of prosperous cities and major empires, with the extensive period of inter-cultural interactions impacting Africa's material culture across the arts, architecture and fashion. Through the lenses of Africa's two major trade histories, the trans-Saharan trade and the trans-Atlantic trade, it is possible to conceptualize the history of fashion in precolonial Africa.

A. La Maison des Reines.
B. L'enceinte de la Cour Royale.
C. Son entrée,
D. Divers Palais de cette Cour.
E. Sortie Solemnelle du Roi.
F. Sa Nobleſse á Cheval.
G. Ioueurs d'inſtrumens á Sa Suite.
H. Fous & Nains.
I. Ioueurs d'inſtrumens qui menent des Tigres prives.

Seventeenth-century engraving from Olfert Dapper's *Naukeurige beschrijvinge der Afrikaensche gewesten,* showcasing a majestic procession at the court of the Kingdom of Benin (in present-day Nigeria).

Trans-Saharan trade

Trans-Saharan trade, which began as early as the fifth century, peaked between the eleventh and sixteenth centuries as a result of the Arab invasion of North Africa, and the patronage of adept Islamic merchants. The trans-Saharan trade networks, which originated in North Africa and penetrated the rainforest regions further south consisted of large caravans of mostly Berber and Andalusian Moor traders. The primary commodities of the outbound trade, gold and slaves – captured through tribal strife and wars – were essential to the northern kingdoms, which traded with distant civilizations including the Levant (western Asia) and Europe. To ensure the safe transit of goods and merchants, entrepôts along major routes provided security and refreshment while exacting tolls and levies. The port cities of Sijilmasa (in Morocco) and Oualata (in Mauritania) grew in wealth and experienced remarkable socio-cultural transformation.

Beside the primary commodities for exchange, the trade fostered the diffusion of an expansive array of luxury goods such as silk skeins, brocades, damask, Fezzan silks and apparel composed of fine linen and cotton from Europe and Egypt. The trade placed within the reach of local artisans new markets, improved technology, novel materials and, in some cases, skilled artisans, which greatly propelled indigenous textile industries. Kofar Mata in Kano, present-day northern Nigeria, for example, was the source of natural indigo-dye fabrics for the nomadic tribes of North Africa, including the Tuaregs and Fulani of Mali. Among the Zazzau (of present-day Kaduna State in Nigeria), an extensive textile and apparel value chain emerged, comprising cotton cultivation, spinning, weaving, dyeing, tailoring and embroidery. The Girken Zazzau and Yar Madaka, both voluminous and sumptuously embroidered gowns, which became popular exports throughout the Sokoto Caliphate and Sudan were the handiwork of master weavers and embroiderers in Kasar Zazzau.

Through trade, new socio-cultural, political and religious ideals filtered into African societies. Trade also guaranteed the prosperity of major indigenous empires and the concomitant development of prolific material cultures. Well into the eighteenth century, increased demand for indigenous cotton and textile products transformed large trading and production centres, such as Kano, into net exporters of textile products, a trade that proved more profitable than the budding slave trade. Some notable trading cities that thrived well into the eighteenth century include Djenne and Timbuktu in Mali, Goa in Songhai, Kaya among the Mossi, Salaga in Ghana, Dendi in northern Dahomey, Ife and Kano in Nigeria, many of which became highly stratified societies, characterized by the sumptuous and elitist lifestyles of distant cultures.

Trade caravans arriving from Europe and the Levant through the northern entrepôts bore not only commodities for exchange, but also precious gifts of lavishly embellished clothing, Persian silk and brocade, regal tunics, sumptuous jewellery and articles such as

The Sultan's advisor in magnificent regalia made of shimmering indigo-dyed fabric.

intricately engraved daggers. These items served as gifts from merchants, or the emissaries of kings, as goodwill gestures. Their quality and exoticism inspired and influenced the arts, fashions and craft of the indigenous societies. Fourteenth-century accounts of the majestic Musa I of Mali hint at a profusion of costly garments, some imported, others made locally. Regaled in silk and brocade, the extravagant Musa made a pilgrimage to Mecca in the company of over a thousand slaves and servants bearing precious gifts for rulers of the distant lands to which he travelled. Silk brocade, which refers to both the textile and the technique, is characterized by complex patterns of embossed floral elements interwoven in threads of gold and silver. This technique, and its spectacular products, although particular to the Persian region, had filtered into the royal courts of Africa through trade, where the Peul or Fulani of Mali developed local expertise.

In the detailed accounts of Islamic scholars, the Kings of Ghana, Kaw Kaw and Mali, as well as the nobility of these ancient Kingdoms adopted styles of dress from regions involved in the trans-Saharan trade, particularly Morocco. The evolution of kente (see p. 38), which is rooted in the panolply of West African strip-weaving cultures, benefited immensely from the flow of colorful silks through the tran-Saharan trade networks encompassing textile hubs in Arabia, Spain and the Fez (in present-day Algeria). Furthermore, trans-Saharan caravans ensured safe passage for itinerant weavers and craftsmen seeking their fortune in new lands where their skill was in high demand.

Trans-Atlantic trade

Trans-Saharan trade thrived well into the late sixteenth century. By the early eighteenth century, however, the trans-Atlantic trade had totally eclipsed the trade networks to the north. The primary objects of this trade were gold, ivory, exotic skins, gum Arabic, spices, and feathers – exchanged for textiles, glass beads, spirits, muskets, sewn garments and many items of luxury – but it differed remarkably from the trans-Saharan trade. Previously, the arduous caravan journeys had restricted the volume and variety of commodities that could be traded, but now the remarkable speed of the seafaring European traders guaranteed access to a greater variety of products, many of which were acquired at entrepôts closer to the West African coast. Again, while the trans-Saharan trade propelled indigenous craft industries, the trans-Atlantic trade undermined them by supplanting indigenous goods, such as local textiles and apparel with an array of imported subsitutes.

The trans-Atlantic trade impacted most profoundly on the socio-cultural and economic fabric of sub-Saharan Africa. Almost as quickly as it began, a vast discovery of European goods entered into the material culture of indigenous societies. However, it was the trade in slaves that ushered in the most unprecedented changes in the socio-economic fabric of sub-Saharan Africa. By the mid-eighteenth century, a surge in the demand for slaves in the Americas and the British West Indies fostered new structures in local trade networks, with intermediary African agents benefiting immensely. Along the 'Slave Coast', in cities such as Lagos, Ane´ho, Porto Novo, Anomabo, Cape Coast and Elmina, intermediary merchant

The salt cellar carved out of ivory by Benin master craftsmen. The cellar portrays Portuguese traders, illustrated with long hair, beards and prominent noses. Atop the sculpture is a Portuguese ship. From Benin, Nigeria, c1525-1600, British Museum, London.

princes also known as 'caboceers' (derived from the Portuguese *caboceiro*, meaning headman or official) wielded substantial influence and power as overlords of the coastal trade. They accumulated immense wealth not only as brokers but as landlords to whom European traders paid rental charges and accorded lavish gifts of clothing and luxury goods.

The goods that appear in thousands of surviving cargo from the mid-eighteenth-century manifestos and order sheets include textiles such as chintz, damask, taffeta, Indian silks, brocade and velvets. Garments from European and British merchants included admiral's coats, hats, shirts, jackets, cloaks, neckties, belts, gloves, stockings, slippers and shoes. There were also household items, and toiletries such as soaps and perfumes. A substantial portion of these goods were intended as supplies for the European crews of slave ships or for circulation only among the elite 'merchant princes' on the coast – as Thomas Melvil, governor of the British settlements on the Gold Coast (1751–6), observed 'the country is full of goods and there is very little demand for anything'.[2]

Culture

Although the precise number is unknown, Africa is inhabited by several thousand different societies and ethnic groups with diverse cultures. In many pre-colonial African societies such as the Berber in the North, the Mande of the Sahel, and Akan of the forest regions, social order and cohesion prevailed around the agency of kingship, divinity and community. Through these agencies, customs and norms were established to govern social life and the transitional stages of birth, puberty, marriage and death. For each of these important events, dress played a significant role, distinguishing between age, occupation, marital status and social class among people of the same community.

Dress continues to be a focal point of festivals and rites of passage in many cultures. Among the Ngoni of Zambia, the paramount chief wears a lion skin during the N'cwala ceremony to celebrate the gift of first fruits. His warriors appear in an array of leopard, cheetah and antelope skins, either draped across their chests or hung around their waists in strips. The Kingdom of Swaziland provides a striking example of the resilience of an African culture, The Swazi cloth, in varying shades of red, is held together with knots and remains a dominant spectacle in contemporary Swaziland at celebrations such as the popular reed dance. Similarly, the ceremonial attire of the town chiefs of Edo State in Nigeria, a spectacular red costume, scalloped on the edges to mimic the scales of the pangolin (which symbolizes the resilience and domineering spirit of the mysterious mammal), is a captivating spectacle at the confluence of culture and dress. Another example of a rich cultural heritage preserved amid the pervading influence of western culture is the Dipo initiation rites among the Krobo of Ghana.

The ceremonial clothes of traditional priests and adherents of traditional African religions were composed of readily available materials such as bark cloth and animal hide. These were embellished with accessories of ivory, bones, cowries, coral shells and seeds. Tribal masks, and a repertoire of headwear and amulets, which are imbued with mystical powers, completed the ensemble in some cultures. The *Sumanbrafo* priests of the Ashanti cover themselves with red clay and black charcoal to project the fierceness of their deity, White cloaks, white chalk and kaolin, which

Armed palace executioner 'Abrafour' wearing a traditional headdress made with cowhide and amulets. Strapped around his waist is a knife sheath made from leopard skin.

signify purity, adorn the priests of the oracle in many African cultures. In Zimbabwe, the Retso cloth, revered for its mystic powers, is still popular among traditional priests and diviners. The red printed textile, with black-and-white geometric patterns, is believed to be a portal into the world of the spirits of ancestors. Masks and masquerades were yet another dominant feature of African ceremonial ensemble.

Throughout Africa's enduring trade relations with the rest of the world, inhabitants of the continent have interacted with foreign cultures, assimilating certain norms. However this assimilation has been subject to the distilling agencies of culture. For instance, through the symbolism and meanings

associated with colour and certain shapes or patterns, a foreign object could be adapted, retain or lose its meaning. In the evocative beading culture of Central and Southern Africa, the Maasai, Dinka, Zulu and Xhosa use extensive terminology drawn from the colour of livestock to describe the appearance and use of imported beads. Among the Akan of Ghana, red symbolizes loss and tragedy and is suited to mourning, whereas blue and white symbolize purity and victory and appropriate for engagement and naming ceremonies. These symbolisms remain relevant in many African cultures, while the phenomenon of adapting foreign objects through an indigenous cultural lens has been termed 'cultural authentication'.

Colonialism

Europe's grand imperialist venture in Africa from the late eighteenth century into the twentieth century remains a defining phenomenon in African history. While parts of Africa had experienced colonization under a succession of foreign powers, European colonization constitutes the most recent, and enduring, influence on the socio-economic, political and cultural fabric of Africa.

The inhabitants of the continent, especially Africans south of the Sahara, bore the brunt of this policy of colonization, involving the callous delineation of colonies with little regard for the traditional monarchies, chiefdoms, disparate cultures and natural borders that had existed since antiquity.

Among the many devices of colonialism, dress constituted, perhaps, the most potent medium of acculturation, as European fashion styles characterized colonies to varying degrees. New clothing norms were introduced subtly through the activities of Christian missionaries, or aggressively through local law-enforcement agencies and pernicious policies such as cotton imperialism – a policy regime that was implemented to undermine the production capacities of indigenous textile industries and favour imported textiles. In West Africa, pioneering Christian missions, such as the Basel Mission from Switzerland, made the adoption of Western clothing a prerequisite for participation in Christian services and enrolment in mission schools. Propriety and modesty in adornment became the watchword of all Christian missions, to symbolize the convert's renunciation of 'archaic' norms. In French colonial Africa, the desire to 'civilize' colonial subjects through the powerful agency of clothing was paramount. The French established the most rigorous of colonial

Opposite
Ekoko n'Uteh masqueraders from the Uteh community, wearing red feathered masks, dance to pay homage to the Oba of Benin. The masqueraders wear raffia pods around their ankles, which rattle as they dance.

Right
Herero women of South West Africa (present day Namibia) during German colonial rule in 1904. The group portrait, which was published in the *Berliner Illustrirte Zeitung*, shows women in full length dresses, and uniforms complete with head scarves.

acculturation machineries, going as far as according citizenship rights to Africans who denounced old traditions and embraced French ideals. The Portugese implemented their version of this known as 'assimilação'. However, while clothing proved an essential part of the arsenal of colonialism, it also served as a tool for contesting colonial dictates. Through clothing, new cultural norms were not just assimilated, but also adapted or outrightly rejected.

Resistance to assimilating foreign cultures yielded some rather surprising outcomes. The Siswati in the Southern African Kingdom of Swaziland, for example, refrain from cutting and sewing imported textiles as they would local hides and leathers; instead, they held them in place with knots above the shoulder. In certain parts of South Africa, men wore only a button-down shirt or a pair of trousers separately, but never together, much to the disappointment of the British Nonconformist mission. Young men from Congo Brazzaville also wore their shirts untucked, because the tucked shirt was a white man's convention. In the 1950s, the quest to abolish the hijab in the French colony of Algeria, fanned the most virulent insurgency under the leadership of unassuming female 'conformists' who hid and trafficked weaponry in plain sight of the local enforcement agencies. Ironically,

Opposite
The Congo's Sapeurs sporting two-piece suits, leather boots and winter scarves stroll through a township in Brazzaville. The Sapeurs adapt the lexicon of European style to contest and subvert the unsettling legacy of colonialism.

Right
Students and teachers dancing Zaire during a festival in Kimpese a town in the Democratic Republic of Congo. They are wearing African wax print which is omnipresent in many African countries.

the Sapeurs (from the French 'La Sape', slang for the 'smartly dressed' and an acronym of 'Société des Ambianceurs et des Personnes Élégantes') of Kinshasa and Brazzaville, a sub-culture that emerged in resistance to the Africanization policy of President Mobutu Sese Seko, employs the very object of colonial subjugation in protest and social activism. The Sapeurs, with their sharp suits, ornate accessories, smoking pipes and pocket watches, far from being an ode to colonialism, interrogated identity and sartorial liberty.

Through extensive encounters with Europeans, West Africans appeared most susceptible to new fashions. However, the incorporation of many western ideals were anchored in indigenous traditions. For example, the success of imported textiles from the nineteenth century – especially imitation wax print (above, and pp.26 and 50) – can be attributed to the predilection of West Africans for colourful regalia such as the kente cloth (see p.38). Furthermore, the shifting demography from the older and more conservative population to young adults who had grown up under the influence of missionaries and the colonial machinery gave impetus to such rapid

assimilation of foreign dress styles.

Globalization

Garbed in fugu (an indigenous apparel of northern Ghana) and acutely aware of the semiotics of fashion, the man who would soon become the first president of Ghana, proclaimed independence from British colonial rule. Throughout the much-publicized inauguration event, Dr Kwame Nkrumah adopted a variety of traditional textiles and dress forms such as the kente cloth (see p.38) to proclaim in the most captivating prose what he called the birth of a new African to the admiration of world. With little doubt, Nkrumah's sartorial overtures, bolstered the resolve of his administration and other leaders in Africa to restore endangered traditions and a heritage in peril against the devastating winds of globalization.

Throughout the history of Africa's extensive interaction with foreign cultures, the impact of globalization has permeated the continent, in particular, the textile and apparel industry. However, this impact became most pronounced in the twentieth century, not just because of the integration of people and cultures through travel, media and technology, but also due to the rise in international trade and the emergence of a global supply chain, in which goods and labour are circulated speedily. As a result, the T-shirt and articles of clothing such as the two-piece suit have become staples of Africa's sartorial landscape and an enduring testament to the power of globalization. Another case in point is the imitation 'African' wax print, which takes inspiration from indigenous cultures but are predominantly of European and Asian origin. The history of imitation wax print, formed at the confluence of globalization, cultural appropriation and colonialization evokes ambivalence.

Despite the pervasiveness of European styles in Africa in the mid-1960s, the collusion of western forms and local tastes allowed for a hybridity of African and European aesthetics: shirts, dresses and dinner gowns made from imitation wax prints (see p.38) and indigenous

Left
Cabinet ministers of the Ghanaian parliament. Seated in the middle is Osagyefo Dr Kwame Nkrumah, Ghana's first president. 17 July 1956.

Opposite
Osibisa, the legendary Afro-Caribbean rock band that held the world spellbound with their soulful and ecstatic music and suave fashions.

textiles readily replaced bland cotton shirts and blouses. In the absence of professional fashion designers, missionary-trained seamstresses and tailors specialized in mending old clothes and creating custom styles based on trendy fashion magazines. Africa's post-colonial decades saw a profusion of fashion styles heavily influenced by western pop culture, entertainment and ecstatic political and social movements – from The Jackson 5 and their signature Afro hair and bell-bottom pants, to the uber-cool Beatles and the sophisticated looks of President John F.

Kennedy, fashion inspiration was everywhere. The Afro-rock band Osibisa swept the globe with their feel-good music and colourful regalia: a fusion of styles in which indigenous African textiles dominate.

Globalization also became an impactful force on the practice of pioneering African designers, many of whom trained in prestigious fashion schools in Europe (See pp. 64-72).

Furthermore, it made geographical location immaterial in categorizing the African designer, as 'living in a diaspora may draw some

designers closer to their African heritage'.[3] An often-cited example is the late Yves Saint Laurent, the Algerian-born French designer who romanticized his North African origins. A prodigy of the twentieth century, Saint Laurent did not shy away from projecting Africa, through captivating collections such as the Andy Warhol-inspired African collection (1967), the Safari (1968) and the Moroccan (1970). He spent much of his final years in Morocco, where his legacy lives on at the Musée Yves Saint Laurent.

Six Yves Saint Laurent designs in homage to Bambara art. SS 67 haute couture collection. Centre Pompidou, Paris, January 22, 2002.

Beyond Africa

Plagued by the paradoxical 'resource curse', Africa is home to almost every known mineral and precious metal and yet has enjoyed less economic growth than regions blessed with fewer natural resources. Raw materials such as agricultural products, timber and rubber, which remain essential to the global luxury economy, abound on the continent. For all of its sturdiness, the Okoume tree, for example, served as the choicest wood for producing Louis Vuitton trunks throughout the nineteenth century. In jewellery, Africa's contribution as a source of precious stones to the value chain of the luxury economy cannot be over-emphasized. Indeed, since the inception of trans-Saharan trade, gold from mines in West and Southern Africa have fed global markets and adorned everything from thrones to robes, precious jewellery and exquisite furniture across Western civilization.

Jutta Wimmler's seminal work of 2017, *The Sun King's Atlantic*, investigates the rarely explored trading activities between West Africa and France in the seventeenth and eighteenth centuries.[4] It argues that the range and volume of materials such as ivory, hardwoods, dyestuffs and gum Arabic imported into France during the bountiful age of French culture and art spurred local craft industries and fuelled the growth of the luxury goods industry in Europe. The Sun King, Louis XIV (r.1643–1715), aided by his trusted minister Jean-Baptiste Colbert, after whom the syndicate of French couturiers, the Comité Colbert, is named, presided over the most elaborate international trade and cultural policy ever known in Europe. During this era, France became a fashion hub, as Europe looked to Paris for the latest styles in dress and fashion etiquette. This renaissance of French culture and the arts under Louis XIV benefited immensely from a range of commodities that originated from its Atlantic trade, specifically from the Senegambia, the region lying between the Senegal River in the north and the Gambia River to the south.

From the African coast across the Atlantic, France and the rest of Europe obtained gum Arabic, a textile resin that served as an essential thickening agent, used with mordants and dyestuffs in the French textile industry. This vital ingredient helped France, and Europe generally, to participate in the transition to using a wider range of artificial dyes and colours. Gum Arabic was also vital to the leather industry in Senegambia, where it was applied to goatskins to improve their quality and lustre, a practice that is believed to have influenced the French tanners who applied it in a similar manner to obtain a brilliant leather sheen. Leather workers in France also administered gum Arabic to damaged hides to restore minor imperfections and perforations. Wimmler opines that readily available natural resources including gold, diamonds, ivory, leather, ambergris, civet (used for musk), wood and the once-indispensable gum Arabic, greatly improved productivity and industrial capacity in Europe, thereby fuelling the democratization of products that were previously the reserve of the wealthy.

African aesthetics in global fashion

Until the late twentieth century when the first generation of ambitious African fashion designers took the couture world by storm (see p.62), the curious and exotic aesthetics of Africa appeared only sporadically in European fashion. Early trends include the *mode à la girafe,* a fashion trend that seized Paris after the presentation of a giraffe by the viceroy of Egypt, Muhammad Ali, to King Charles X of France in 1827.

The discovery of Tutankhamun's grave in 1922, and the subsequent global tour of the grave goods, sparked a global trend, known as 'Tutmania'. In haute couture, design stalwart of the Belle Epoque, Paul Poiret's 1920 creation, the Tanger, closely mimicked the akhnif, a cloak originating from Morocco's High Atlas region. Poiret also captured the exoticism of Africa through a series of commissioned textiles from Rodier, a leading French textile manufacturer. Other designers who made a foray into African fashion include Marie-Louise Carven, whose collections in the 1950s comprised dresses, bathing suits and wraps in wax prints, batik and raffia fabrics; Algerian-born Yves Saint Laurent who released a collection of Bambara dresses in 1967 (inspired by the sculptures produced by the community of the same name in Mali, see p.28) and Missoni with its Africa di Missoni collection in the 1990s.[5]

Besides couture catwalks, African fashion permeated western culture though migration and informal trade networks. For example, the dashiki, a loose-fitting tunic made of either woven or printed textile, arrived in the United States in the luggage of Peace Corps volunteers returning from Africa. The dashiki was further popularized through film, Afro-pop and rock music, and symbolized the irreverence for orthodox fashion in the hippie era. Beyond the trend, the dashiki, along with a vast repertoire of ankara-print dresses, embroidered boubous, and Afro hair lent identity to the black nationalist movements of the 1960s. They persist as visible clothing items in many African American communities across the United States to this day.

Furthermore, the evergreen animal print craze, inspired by the skin costumes of African royalty, pervades global fashion. Leopard frocks, the stripes of the zebra and tiger and even the spots of the hyena continue to be in vogue.

Opposite

Mode à la girafe – giraffe-
inspired fashion of the
late-1820s France. The
arrival of the curious exotic
animal inspired thousands
of prints, toys, pamphlets,
ceramic wares, fashion and
even food. This episode
was, however, not the first.
In 1749 there had been a
mode au rhinocéros and a
mode au zèbre in 1786. From
*Le journal des dames et des
modes*, 25 June 1827.

Right

Marie-Louise Carven,
design for the summer 1949
collection. This design for a
dress is labelled 'Afrique'.

A Textile Heritage

∿∿∿∿∿∿∿∿∿∿

Throughout history, textiles have served as a medium for communicating and preserving African culture and traditions. Far beyond their utility, textiles constitute a craft and an art form: through the evocative patterns, symbols and motifs of copious African textiles, pivotal events were recorded, legends were immortalized, religious beliefs and customs, as well as family legacies, were entrenched.

A wide variety of indigenous textiles and clothing composed of cotton, raffia, silk and wool have circulated widely in Africa since antiquity. Archaeological excavations have found cotton textiles in Nubia that are dated between the first and seventh centuries, while eleventh century accounts of the Kingdom of Takrur in Northern Senegal attest to a vibrant textile economy with many houses having their own 'cotton tree'. Evidence of weaving in Africa includes the discovery of small ceramic spindle whorls in areas such as Mauretania, Senegal, Guinea, Mali and northern Ghana.

Africa's deep rooted textile economy is expansive and diverse, fostered through an interconnected network of weavers, consumers and traders both indigenous and foreign. Bustling textile markets in any of Africa's cosmopolitan marketplaces reveal to the curious consumer a vast range of woven, dyed, stamped and printed cloth, some handwoven and others printed in industrial mills. The textiles differ according to the fibre used, the dyeing procedure employed and the composition of dyes, whether natural or synthetic. Recently, advanced printing techniques have spurred considerable variety in surface designs and finishing, placing at the disposal of contemporary designers a range of African, or African-inspired fabrics in silk, chiffon and organza. Despite the threat of cheap textile imports, many of Africa's handwoven indigenous textiles prevail in a testament to the resilience of the cultures that produce them.

Kuba dancer in woven raffia skirt, Democratic Republic of Congo. Cut-pile Kuba cloth, worn by chiefs or men of high rank, indicates their status within Kuba society.

Woven stories and ancient fabrics

African textile history is as rich and evocative as the textiles themselves. The earliest forms of clothing in prehistoric Africa included materials such as the bark of trees, leather hides from game and girdles made of fibre from raffia palm. In the royal tombs of Ancient Egypt, aprons, cloaks, penis sheaths and sandals made from leather, papyrus, linen and palm fibre have been preserved.

Linen, made from flax, was the dominant textile for clothing, bed covers and mummy wrappings. The finest yarns produced a more luxuriant texture for manufacturing shirts, dresses, gowns and tunics. Linen tunics were stamped with geometric motifs or embellished with golden accessories and semi-precious stones to indicate the status of its wearers. The Nubian Kingdom, immediately south of Egypt, also utilized leather in the production of loincloths, skirts, girdles, sandals and hats.

Historians and archaeologists have established the existence of a wholly indigenous African textile industry, albeit with significant influences from cultures across the Mediterranean. In North Africa, invading global powers, including the Persian, Greek, Phoenician, Roman and the Arab greatly shaped the textile heritage of the region. In West Africa, the comparatively limited interaction with other cultures fostered the development of a vibrant and truly independent textile economy. Among the vast repertoire of weaving techniques, strip weaving has the longest history in Africa, with evidence found in the Tellem caves of Mali. The strip cloth, woven on rudimentary single- or double-heddle looms was either sewn together to form a wider piece of cloth or used as a currency in bartering goods. While the origins and historic development of African looms and weaving technology are unclear, historians have established a connection between indigenous African looms and Asiatic or Middle Eastern looms for their striking semblance. It is probable, however, that many African looms have undergone significant modifications to suit the local context.

For centuries, the centres of textile excellence were connected through trade, with the vast network of ancient production and trading hubs spanning Sanga and Kumbi-Saleh in Mali, Tegdaoust in Mauritania, Ogo in the Kingdom of Takrur in present-day Senegal, Kano in Nigeria and Niani in Guinea. Each region of Africa exhibited proficiency in the use of materials such as flax, wool, wild silk, cotton, raffia and bast fibres. For example, while cotton weaving was commonplace, the indigenous production of woven silk was restricted mainly to Nigeria, where silk yarn was obtained from a species of wild moth known as the Anaphe. In Mali, where cotton abounds, funerary clothing excavated from the Bandiagara Escarpment, underscores its use as the choice material for tunics, hats and loincloths. The Kuba of Congo are also known for their mastery of the raffia fibre.

Through trade and the practice of itinerant weavers, the textile industry was greatly influenced by both indigenous and foreign cultures. The Peul or Fulani in Mali mastered the intricate technique of brocading, a mainstay technique of the Andalusian Moors. Imported garments with intricate embroidery

A kente weaver using
a single-heddle
horizontal loom.

and colourful brocaded motifs interspersed
were not only valuable gifts for monarchs, but a
reference point for local craftsmanship. From
the seventeenth century onwards, the woven
silk textiles of the Ashanti and Ewe tribes were
made by unravelling the yarns of silk cloth that
trickled down through the trans-Saharan trade.
Despite the relative simplicity and rudimentary

nature of the single- and double-heddle looms,
intricate textiles such as the Shoowa cloth, the
kente, the aso-oke and the akotifahana were
woven. These are briefly explored in the
following sections.

Shoowa

The people of ancient Anziku Kingdom, which
stretched across present-day Gabon, the
Republic of Congo and the Democratic
Republic of Congo, made elaborate cloths from
raffia fibre, jewellery and special insignia to
denote membership of prestigious families.
European travellers marvelled at the quality and
excellent finish of the raffia cloth, likening it to
velvet, taffeta, satin and damask. The
spectacular Shoowa cloth (also known as Kuba
cloth after the Kuba Kingdom) has traditionally
been produced by both men and women
artisans. The weaving process begins with the
harvesting, stripping, drying and beating of the
raffia palm to extract the fibres. This is followed
by spinning and weaving, with the preparatory
and weaving stages undertaken primarily by
men. The finished textile may be further
enhanced with appliqué, patchwork or resist
dyeing before being transformed into bags,
clothing and decorative objects. The elaborate
secondary procedures are undertaken by
women, who exhibit profound skill in cut-pile
embroidery, tufting and patchwork. The result
is a distinctive textile in bold, earthy colours
with a velvety feel.

A variety of handwoven cut-and-pile Shoowa/ Kuba cloth.

The traditional weaving technique is embedded with geometric patterns and a variety of tactile effects created from different pile-and-cut techniques.

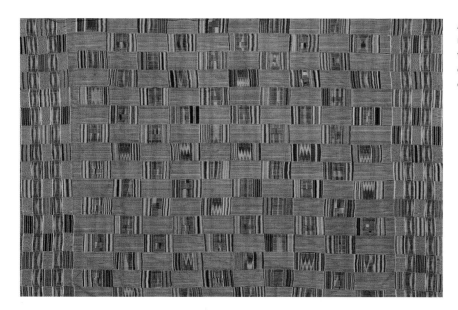

A variant of the intricate royal Ashanti kente cloth, woven with unravelled yarns of imported silk cloth, c.1920s-1940.

Kente

The masterfully woven kente cloth of the precolonial West African kingdom of Ashanti is renowned globally. Its origin is shrouded in mystery, with folklore attributing its invention to a hunter's attempt to imitate the pattern of a spider's web. Archaeological findings place hinge its origins to the strip-weaving cultures of West Africa dating to the eleventh century, and it is believed to have been shaped by access to raw materials, skilled artisans and improved technology under the impetus of trade.

Kente serves as a prestigious ceremonial cloth and is produced in a variety of finishes for the highly stratified Ashanti society. To maintain its allure, kente in Ancient Ashanti was governed by sumptuary laws throughout the eighteenth century that prevented its vulgarization. Furthermore, the most exclusive variant of the kente cloth, known as adweneasa (the pinnacle of creativity), was produced by the master craftsmen for the king. The standards of weaving were exacting, requiring the oversight of the King's specially appointed kente chiefs also known as the Kentehene. The technique for the production of the king's exclusive cloth was kept secret, making it a punishable offence for a commoner to wear or display in public the same exclusive design as the king. Under the patronage of the prominent King Opoku Ware I (1700-1750), kente weaving entered a golden age as he nurtured and promoted the exploits of the guild of kente weavers at Bonwire. His court comprised a guild of skilled weavers who worked with a bewildering variety of colourful silk and taffeta yarns, with imported silks from Fezzan and red taffetas from Italy and France forming the foundation of the Ashanti strip-weaving culture.

A contemporary adaptation of the Yoruba aso-oke by Kenneth Ize showcased during Arise Fashion week in Lagos, Nigeria in 2019.

In ancient times, induction into the guild of weavers at Bonwire was by pedigree, ensuring that craftsmen were nurtured by a preceding generation of distinguished master craftsmen. Today, despite soaring sales over the past few decades, the craft has declined steadily in quality and prestige. The resilient and lustrous silk yarns have been replaced with rayon, resulting in a product that is more pliant and readily available. The kente cloth has also been democratized and is no longer the reserve of Ashanti elite. Nevertheless, kente is still valuable in Ghanaian and African culture. It is used for important occasions such as marriage ceremonies, festivals and stately events. During festivals and major traditional ceremonies, prominent chiefs are carried aloft in palanquins wearing kente and adorned in sumptuous gold regalia, such as armlets, anklets, necklaces, sandals and staffs. Beyond the borders of Ghana, kente is an enduring symbol of empowerment and identity in the African diaspora. The symbolic gesture of Democrat members of congress who, in solidarity with the Black Lives Matter movement, knelt at the US Capitol with kente stoles around their necks is rooted in this ideal.

Aso-oke

Tailored and worn in a variety of forms of garment, or used as a headwrap (gele), aso-ilu-oke is a staple of Nigeria's elite and aspired to by its expanding middle class. The ancient handwoven textile, known popularly as aso-oke, was originally introduced in Yorubaland, West Africa, in the fifteenth century. *Aso* is a Yoruba word for cloth and symbolizes the respect and dignity that is accorded a well-dressed person. While the Yoruba culture is replete with admirable textile crafts, such as the sanyan (made with indigenous silk), the alaari baba aso, a delicately textured cloth, woven in red, and the etu aso agba (deep-blue, indigo-dyed cloth) among others, the aso-oke meaning 'top cloth' is the most prestigious of all.

Aso-oke, like kente cloth, derives its prestige from symbolic colours and elaborate patterns, which are imbued with cultural meaning. The process of weaving commences with the harvesting and spinning of cotton into yarns, then the yarns are dyed, woven in strips on a double heddle before being sewn together into large fabrics. Aso-oke is used on special occasions and has experienced a resurgence among Nigerian millennials as the go-to textile for traditional marriage ceremonies. The textile has also enjoyed remarkable exposure through music and film, especially through Nollywood – Nigeria's multibillion-dollar cinema industry. Aso-oke is popular among the Yoruba and, for many Nigerians in the diaspora, it is perpetually relevant as a vector of cultural identity and heritage. Kenneth Ize, LVMH's 2019 finalist (see p.38), whose work comprises an astonishing range of aso-oke garments, belongs to a generation of culturally conscious and ethically driven designers in the global marketplace.

Akotifahana

In contrast to the well-documented textile cultures of West Africa and North Africa, woven textiles in Southern Africa are rarely explored. A particular example is the captivating textile culture of the Merina people in the central highlands of the island of Madagascar, which is home to almost thirteen known varieties of locally grown silks. Indeed, Merina weavers

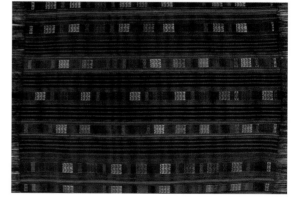

Variants of the akotifahana woven by the Merina people in the central highlands of Madagascar. A highly detailed finish attests to the dexterity of master craftswomen in the use of cotton, wild silk, hemp and weaver's banana. These cloths are all woven from silk.

produce a wide variety of textiles, from luxury silks to common bast and leaf loincloths, the most prestigious of which is akotofahana/akotifahana, an intricately woven silk brocade with origins in the early eighteenth century. The textile, which is usually woven with imported silk, was the preserve of kings and the noble class, and a venerated gift for high-ranking officials and foreign dignitaries. European traders and colonial officials, fascinated by its luxurious texture, compared it to beautiful antique cashmere.[6] Akotifahana was woven by the most skilled and innovative Merina women, who exhibited a remarkable proficiency in the use of cotton, wild silk, hemp, weaver's banana and Chinese silk, and embodies influences from India and the southern part of the Arabian Peninsula, which shared strong commercial ties with the island. The deep intermingling of the island's multicultural inhabitants, which include Indonesian, Bantu, Swahili, Indian, Arab and European migrants, is evident in the complex patterns of the textile. Like other African textiles, akotifahana has been influenced by a profusion of imported fibres, dyes and patterns.

Other distinguished weaving crafts

Weaving and textile crafts in Africa are as diverse and complex as the cultures of the continent, making it nearly impossible to capture them all in one single volume. Nevertheless, a few more distinctive and intriguing textile traditions bear mentioning. First, is the cloth of the Manjak, a tribe that is scattered across the Gambia, Senegal and Guinea-Bissau. The Manjak are believed to have acquired the weaving skill while in captivity on the island of Cape Verde. The Manjak fabric has a distinctive geometric pattern that may resemble the kente cloth, however, the cloth is supple and versatile to a wide range of uses. Contemporary designers Adama Paris and Aissa Dione are foremost proponents of its revival and preservation. Another textile of interest is the Gonja cloth, a strip-woven textile craft common to the northern region of Ghana. Gonja cloth is used in the production of smocks (worn with a matching cap and also featuring embroidery and appliqué designs made to suit the rank and prestige of its wearers), batakari or fugu (both derivatives of smocks, made only for kings, traditional leaders and priests of the Sahel region). However, despite its wide adoption among people of different regions and faith in West Africa, Gonja cloth – with its origins in the predominantly Muslim northern Ghana – has become synonymous with Islam.

Another valuable ancient textile craft, which originates from Igboland (in present-day southeastern Nigeria) and is deemed to be as old as the Igbo nation, is the Akwete textile. Unlike kente and aso-oke, Akwete is made on vertical broad looms known as the *nkwe,* which makes the production of wide fabrics possible. The textile, with its visually striking and evocative motifs and patterns, is believed, as so many others, to have entered cultures in North Africa via trans-Saharan trade and to have benefited from the inflow of novel materials. The evocative patterns and brilliant colours of Akwete cloth are symbolic, and were in ancient times governed by strict sumptuary laws. For example, the tortoise motif (or *ikaki*) was the preserve of the royal and noble class and was

Manjak

Top to bottom
Quittah cloth made by
Manjako in Guinea-Bissau.
Made of silk and cotton.

Manjaka woman's wrapper
(Seru Njaago).

Akwete cloth in the *ikaki*
tortoise pattern. It is made
by Igbo in Nigeria and is
woven from cotton.

prohibited among commoners. The enigmatic ebe design was also restricted to warriors, hunters and pregnant women as it bore patterns to confound evil spirits. Akwete has been popularized since the 1990s through the patronage of personalities and royalty – notably HRH Prince Charles and Diana, Princess of Wales.

The Gonja cloth, a staple for the predominantly Muslim communities of the Sahel Sahara region in West Africa.

Dyeing and printing

Dyeing as a specialist craft has been a key component of Africa's textile traditions. Locally produced or imported textiles were dyed with a range of organic and vegetable dyes sourced from plants and the barks of trees. Regional variations in dyeing techniques have been underpinned by a variety of factors, the most important of which has been the ingenuity of indigenous craftsmen and access to imported dyes at the onset of the trans-Atlantic trade. The most popular techniques of dyeing and printing include resist dyeing, stamping, screen printing and, in recent decades, industrial imitation wax printing.

Resist dyeing

Resist dyeing is by far the most popular dyeing technique in Africa. This technique is both basic and intuitive offering ample room for experimentation and success, even for novices. The technique that is popular in other parts of the world involves the process of blocking parts of the textile from absorbing dyes, either through tying, as well as stamping and drawing with resist mediums including starch and wax. The types of fabrics produced with this technique include the adire, the boglanfini, the batik and the Adinkra cloth.

Adire In West Africa, the Yoruba of southwestern Nigeria are known for a traditional resist-dye technique used to produce the indigo adire fabrics. Traditionally, adire is created using an entirely organic process, commencing with the harvesting and processing of the indigo-bearing elu plant. The dye solution is created from the ashes of dried cocoa shells, into which the dried and pummelled Elu leaves are immersed. The next stage – preparing the fabric for dyeing – determines the type of adire produced: when the resisting agent is raffia, iko, and tying and stitching patterns, the outcome is adire oniko. Alternatively, the application of starch or wax produces the variant adire eleko. The adire technique is

Opposite
Patterns in adire cloth created by wax resist technique.

Opposite left
Adire Oniko, made by tying with raffia or stitching threads to create patterns.

Opposite right
Adire eleko, made by stamping wax-resist patterns onto cotton cloth.

Above
The dye pits of Kofar Mata, an ancient dyeing community in Kano, the northern part of Nigeria.

similar to the tie-dye method employed by textile artisans across many West African countries, such as Ghana, Ivory Coast and Senegal. However, while synthetic dyes have become commonplace in batik and tie-dyeing, traditional adire remains distinguished by its use of organic indigo and elu dyes.

Organic indigo dyeing, the technique by which adire is produced, requires exacting skills as it relies on living bacteria to extract pigment from the leaves of the indigo plant. Adire, with its captivating blue hues and luminescent motifs, was, for centuries, a status symbol that was highly prized among the Tuareg nomads. The textile, which featured as a prominent commodity of the trans-Saharan trade, originated from the dye pits of Kofar Mata in northern Nigeria, where it has been produced for nearly five centuries. Craftsmen in Kofar Mata have sustained the use of organic dyes and remain loyal to the ancient technique of indigo dyeing. Indigo dyeing is also commonplace among the Sahel region of Mali and Guinea, a tradition that has seen a revival under the patronage of globally acclaimed textile artist and designer Aboubakar Fofana.

Bogolanfini, which literary means 'mud cloth', is made by assembling into one cloth numerous strips of hand-spun cotton. The cotton cloth is resist-dyed using a vegetable dye and a mud solution. The resist dyeing technique of the Bamana people is, however, unusual. Traditionally, bogolanfini begins by soaking the cotton cloth in a mulch of indigenous leaves, resulting in a deep yellow colour. Intricate patterns are drawn, using mud collected from the bottom of local rivers, which has been stored for a year or more to enrich its potency. The cloth is allowed to dry, causing a chemical reaction between the iron oxide in the mud and the tannic acid from the local leaves to produce a deep hue of black, which forms the background of the design. The mud is washed off and the yellow mordant is discharged with caustic soda.

This meticulous and labour-intensive procedure relies on the oxidization of mineral deposits in the mud which produces a rustic finish with unique shades of brown, golden yellow and off-white. The geometric patterns of the bogolanfini and the process of dyeing,

Above
The mud cloth, also known as bogolanfini, developed by the Mande people of Mali. This cloth more specifically is made by Bamana people.

Opposite
A master artist hand paints patterns with mud on indigenous cotton fabric.

which relies on elements of nature, is believed to imbue the garment with special protective powers. The superstition associated with the potency of bogolanfini has popularized its use among hunters and traditional leaders in Mali and Guinea. Pioneering Malian designer Chris Seydou, who contributed immensely to propelling the bogolanfini onto the global stage in the mid-1970s, out of reverence for the traditional textile found it difficult to cut the bogolanfini.

Batik The technique of batik has been practised in Africa for over a century. However, its origin and introduction to Africa is contested. Evidence of batik, a wax-resist dyeing technique, has been traced to the Middle East, Central Asia and India, with the most conceivable assumption hinting to its movement across the Mediterranean through the channels of the trans-Saharan trade. The process of batiking involves the stamping of patterns on cotton using wax, or cassava starch, as a resist before being submerged in a dye solution. Unlike adire, which is limited to a monochrome pattern, batiking permits multiple stamping and dyeing to produce multicoloured textiles. Batik dyeing received a boost at the introduction of synthetic dyes in the twentieth century; however, the popularity of the original craft has waned due to the invasion of factory-printed variants of imitation wax print and imports from China since the nineteenth century.

Stamped Cloth

Although stamping is employed as a technique in resist dyeing, it is also applicable as a standalone procedure in the production of textiles. Stamping and printing in such circumstances are direct mediums by which dyes and colours are affixed to textiles. In this process, motifs were carved in relief on stamps that were improvised from everyday objects such as gourds and pieces of wood. Before the introduction of industrial printed textiles, the most popular stamped and printed textiles included the Adinkra cloth of the Akan in Ghana,

the huronko in Sierra Leone and a variety of stamped cloth found in Guinea and Mali.

Adinkra cloth follows in prestige only to kente cloth. However, its prestige stems neither from the intricacy of its patterns nor the laboriousness of the procedure but as a textile of special ceremonial significance. Made using a paste-resist technique, Adinkra cloth was imprinted with sacred symbols and served primarily as a mourning cloth. The earliest known Adinkra cloth, housed in the British Museum, is believed to have been produced in 1817. Adinkra, from which the cloth has its name, refers to a collection of ancient and sacred symbols that are used in ancestral worship. It was originally the preserve of royals and nobility, and was produced in limited

Left
Stamped Adinkra cloth with meticulously rendered lines and patterns.

Right
The stamping procedure, dyed on fabric with original colour is stamped using embossed wooden stamps.

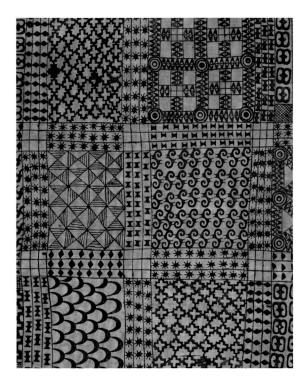

Mourners wearing
stamped Adinkra cloth
during a funeral event.

colours, with each chromatic scheme
determining its purpose. Black and red, for
example, symbolized loss and grief and
appeared most appropriate for mourning and
funeral ceremonies. White, on the contrary,
symbolized victory or joy and was used for
initiation rites or naming ceremonies. The
production of Adinkra cloth involves dyeing
the base textile and then stamping Adinkra
symbols using gourd stamps and organic

dyes. Akin to traditional adire, Adinkra only
uses organic dyes produced from the bark of
the *Bade3* (an indigenous tree species) and the
root of the kuntunkuni tree. There has been a
sharp decline in the use of traditional Adinkra
cloth, with marked iterations to the technique.
Screen printing has replaced stamping and the
dyes wih water-based acrylic paints. Industrial
printed variants have also contributed to the
sharp decline.

Opposite
The display of pomp and pageantry at the 25th anniversary of the Asantehene (Ashanti King). The Chief sword bearer wears an amulet headdress comprising a Ram horn and feathers detailed with gold-encrusted jewellery.

Top
A meticulously rendered gold armband made by indigenous Senegalese metalsmiths for the signares.

This bracelet style, popular in the 1920s, was inspired by Roman gladiators' wristbands. This particular cuff, however, was made in the 1940s or '50s, when the style resurfaced in honour of Lamine Guèye, a politician who supported women's suffrage.

Right
1979 engraving showing, second from left, a Signare from Saint Louis, Senegal.

In most societies, the dominant material for jewellery depended on its availability, as well as the skillset of craftsmen and the social-cultural beliefs surrounding its use. In the cultures of Northern Africa where Islamic influence was strong, silver was favoured above gold for its purity and modest appeal. Gold was, however, the mineral of choice among the Akan in West Africa, while the bronze guilds of Benin became popular for their dexterity with brass. There were, moreover, specific crafts to which the entire existence of the craftsman was dedicated. This was the case among the Mande tribe of Guinea and Mali, where blacksmiths held a special, almost mythical, status. The blacksmith devoted his life and his craft to the service of the gods and the king. They were revered for possessing disruptive knowledge and power and were confined to the outskirts of the community. Consequently, a caste, formed from the lineage of craftsmen emerged.

In eighteenth-century Senegal, a special caste of master craftsmen plied their trade under the patronage of wealthy women known as signares (from the Portuguese 'senhora' for 'lady'). The story of these powerful ladies, who appropriated the semiotics of jewellery for prestige and fame borders on the sumptuous dynamics of luxury in Africa. The expert goldsmiths executed a variety of magnificent pieces, which were meticulously worked into fascinating shapes and tiny, near-impossible, filigreed-wire effects. The wealthiest signares established ateliers on the ground floor of their houses where they employed goldsmiths and seamstresses to fulfil their custom demands.

Beading

Beading is deeply rooted in the history of Africa. Indeed, before the introduction of imported glass beads, various kinds of woven textiles, bark cloth and hides were embellished with beads made from ostrich egg shells, seeds, obsidian or marine shells. In North Africa, evidence of faience (sintered quartz) beads, produced entirely by hand, exist in ancient Egyptian tomb paintings that date to 4000 BC. And clothing artefacts sumptuously embellished with ostrich eggshells have been found in pre-dynastic Egyptian burial sites.

While this heritage endures throughout the continent, some cultures exhibited exceptional mastery of the craft. Examples include the Zulu, the Ndebele, the Sotho and Tsonga in Southern Africa; the Maasai, Dinka and Kuba in East Africa; the Yoruba, Igbo, Edo, Ashanti and Krobo in West Africa. In all these cultures, the expansive variety of beads birthed diverse techniques and unique aesthetics.

Beads as items of status also included semi-precious minerals, such as lapis lazuli stones, quartz, agate, electrum, turquoise, steatite, and amazonite (feldspar). In Nigeria, the Ille-Ife terracotta point to an elaborate beading culture, with cylindrical red beads composed of jasper and carnelian stones produced for the royal class. The production of glass beads appears to have been a major industry in Ille Ife as fragments of crucibles employed in the process have been discovered in excavations across the city. In Southern Africa, beading was commonplace, but differed from tribe to tribe in terms of form, texture, motifs, palettes and the materials onto which beading was done. The earliest documented Southern African beading tradition is attributed to the ornamentation among the San tribes, who constructed artefacts from ostrich eggshells strung together with sinew from the shoulders of goats and cows. Archaeologists have traced the network of bead trade from Arikamedu in South India to the Eastern coast of Africa to as far back as 200 BC.[7]

However, glass beads gained prominence in Southern Africa from the eleventh century as they trickled from entrepôts along the coast of Mogadishu, Pemba, Zanzibar Islands, Kilwa, and Sofala and Delagoa Bay in Mozambique. Glass beads became an instant success for their uniformity in size and brilliant colours, sparking a revolution in personal adornment within tribes

Top
Sotho women in beaded
neckpieces, bustiers
and skirts.

Bottom left
Maasai woman in a beaded
disc necklace and beaded
headband. The ensemble is
accentuated with coiled
wristbands made from
brass and iron.

Bottom right
An Edo chief seated at the
Igue ceremony wears a
collar made of agate beads.
Coral necklaces and gourd
armbands complete the
ensemble.

with existing predilections for the craft. Beyond the confluence of trade, its widespread adoption was further propelled by the activities of colonial powers, including the Dutch, Portuguese and English, who assumed control of the region and its trade at various points in time.

From the sixteenth century, bead trade thrived under the patronage of Bantu chiefs, who controlled its distribution among their wives, noblemen and subjects.. The monopoly made them rare and precious, however, by the turn of the twentieth century, its distribution had been democratized through the activities of European traders. Consequently, their widespread adoption and immense socio-cultural and economic importance have made them a fundamental aspect of the region's cultural heritage. Among the Zulus, courting youths used beaded tokens to communicate emotional and esoteric messages, by encoding into the patterns and arrangement of beadwork messages to express affection. Xhosa couples were decked in elaborate bead textiles, complemented with beaded accessories, such as headbands, fringed necklaces, armbands and neckbands. Among the Ndebele, distinctive

types of beadwork, worn with peculiar etiquette was indicative of the woman's maturity. For example, the lighabi, a beaded, fringed apron that is worn around the hips, identifies a very young girl, while an older pubescent girl wears an isiphephetu, a rectangular-shaped apron made of hide or canvas and decorated with geometric beaded patterns.

Many beading traditions have survived under the patronage of indigenous tribes, who despite the overwhelming influence of modern dress styles continuously incorporate beadwork into garments for rites of passage, festivals and marriage ceremonies. Fully beaded costumes are used during festive occasions and have become prized items for museums and the tourist market. The Ndebele people, with their traditional beaded adornments, dress and unique wall paintings, have one of the most renowned African beading cultures. The art and traditional beadwork of the Ndebele has survived through a generation of master craftswomen such as South Africa's foremost cultural evangelist, Dr Esther Mahlangu, who since the 1990s has worked with numerous global brands to promote Ndebele culture.

Ndebele woman in a geometric-patterned, beaded headdress and necklace. She also wears a neck-elongating coil necklace and Basotho blanket.

CHAPTER 2

The New Africa

For the potential of its vast and largely untapped consumer markets, Africa is often seen as the last frontier of the global economy. Fundamental to its improving socio-economic fortune is the steady transition towards good governance, better public infrastructure, economic and political stability.

In this context, Africa's burgeoning middle and upper class have fuelled consumption along the spectrum of the retail economy, including luxury goods. Iconic brands of the LVMH, Kering, Richemont and Estée Lauder groups have established a direct presence in leading economies across the continent. However, African consumers are also turning to indigenous brands. This phenomenon is hinged on the resurgent pride in local culture, arts and crafts, with the continent's diverse and rich heritage constituting valuable touchpoints for the creative economy. Among the plethora of avenues for creativity and culture, fashion constitutes the single most potent medium for individual and collective expression. Consequently, African brands, previously confined to the periphery of the global fashion economy, are invading global media and occupying hallowed spaces in fashion capitals across the globe.

In this chapter the most prolific designers operating from or out of Africa – the 'generation couture' pioneers who made this renaissance possible - are profiled. These profiles are followed by a discussion on the exigencies of developing a truly sustainable fashion and luxury industry with global reach.

Generation Couture

∿∿∿∿∿∿∿∿∿∿∿

Barely recovered from the trauma of World War II, the world witnessed the vivacity of fashion in the so called 'golden age of couture'; an audacious era, punctuated by the defining works of, among others, Christian Dior, Cristóbal Balenciaga, Pierre Balmain. It was in this era, further contextualized by the struggle for independence and smouldering sentiments of pan-Africanism that Africa's pioneering fashion designers emerged.

Naturally, the zeitgeist of the mid-twentieth century prefaced and greatly shaped the practice of Africa's designers, who blazed the trail for the preservation and promotion of African indigenous artforms, crafts and textiles. The canon is replete with designers and creators who galvanized scant resources to revitalize ailing local textile industries. They leveraged their proficiency in couture techniques to reinterpret the bogolanfini, the kente, the aso-oke and adire, showcasing the outcomes both home and abroad. Many of them succeeded in distilling traditional textiles into forms that were compatible with the production of the already pervasive western-style shirts, suits and dresses. They are revered globally as luminaries who contributed invaluably to the reconstruction of the African identity and the globalization of African fashion.

Larissa, Callista and Seren designs from Ethereal Tropical Galactica SS21 collection by Deola Sagoe.

Left
Shade Thomas-Fahm
visiting weavers and
working at the loom. 1960s.

Opposite
Juliana Norteye 'Chez
Julie', Akwadzan, late
1960s, wax print, in the
collection of the Harn
Samuel P. Harn Museum of
Art, University of Florida,
Gainesville. It was shown at
their 2015 'Kabas and
Couture' exhibition.

Folashade Thomas-Fahm

In 1952 a young Thomas-Fahm left Nigeria to train as a nurse in London but, upon arriving, switched to study fashion after encountering the beautiful shopfronts of boutiques in London's West End. She studied fashion at the Barrett Street Technical College (now London College of Fashion), and later at Saint Martin's School of Art (now Central Saint Martins), juggling school with odd jobs including waitressing at Lyons' Corner House. Determined to establish a successful fashion house, Thomas-Fahm returned to Nigeria in 1960 and set up a factory and a boutique. She focused on simplifying and modernizing style for Nigeria's rapidly expanding working class by adapting indigenous textiles such as the aso-oke, adire, and Akwete into contemporary western-style garments. Thomas-Fahm created zippered skirts to mimic indigenous wrappers and adapted the boubou, a traditionally gendered attire to suit women's bodies, while creating beachwear composed of indigenous textiles.[8]

Beyond her passion and creativity, Shade also set the standard for creative enterprise, establishing the first ready-to-wear collection for retail across a chain of Shade Boutiques. Shade operated an integrated value chain, manufacturing locally from her garment factory in Yaba, she felt just as much burdened to create jobs within fashion. In pioneering a truly indigenous fashion business, Shade demonstrated remarkable resilience in the face of overwhelming prejudice and contempt for indigenous textiles. She spearheaded the reclamation of a nation's identity through fashion, and re-oriented mindsets on the creative career of a fashion designer.

Chez Julie

Some 200 nautical miles west of Lagos, and in the bustling cosmopolitan city of Accra, another creative genius would emerge at around the same time as Shade. Juliana 'Chez Julie' Norteye (1933–1993), who had trained at the École Guerre Lavigne (later ESMOD)

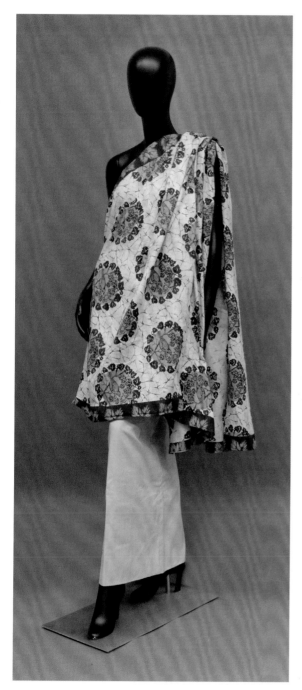

returned to Ghana from Paris in 1961. In the course of the next three decades, Chez Julie became the de-facto fashion icon in the capital city of Accra, hosting prestigious annual fashion shows, collaborating with Ghana's first wax print manufacturing company GTP (Ghana Textile Production), and catering to the sartorial needs of distinguished women, mostly wives of diplomats, first ladies, businesswomen and many others.

Chez Julie is credited with many innovations to Ghanaian traditional style, such as the Kente Kaba, an elegant dinner dress made from kente cloth. The Akwadan, an adaptation of the male toga-style garment (wrapped around the torso and tucked in place at the shoulder), was perhaps the most avant garde of all her creations, as she subverted the gendered garment, deploying subtle and ingenious features to create a modern, versatile and chic garment for the contemporary African woman. In 2016, Norteye's illustrious work was celebrated at the exhibition titled 'Kabas and Couture' at the Harn Museum of Art, at the University of Florida. 'The Queen of Accra Fashion', not only captivated the elite and fashionistas of her era, but also paved the way for the next generation of Ghanaian and African designers.

Oumuo Sy

Like the fashion-forward cities of Lagos and Accra, Dakar offers a vibrant cityscape; one that has for decades served as the stage for the imaginations of Senegal's 'Queen of Couture', Oumuo Sy (b. 1952). Since the 1980s, Sy has manifested her creative prowess across the arts from cinema and theatre to music and dance. In fashion, her theatrical predilection is evident in her outlandish costumes, couture, and

Left
Models present creations by
Senegalese fashion designer Oumou
Sy, during the 10th Dakar Fashion
Week on June 15, 2012.

unconventional jewellery accessories.

Unlike many of her contemporaries, Sy had neither a formal education nor training in fashion. However, she received her first sewing machine at the age of thirteen and she started piecing together recuperated fabrics to make garments from an early age. She went on to study art and began her career in cinema. As a costumier, Sy encountered many career highlights including creating the wardrobe for Djibril Diop Mambéty's social satire *Hyenas*.

Sy merges indigenous textiles, traditional artforms and impeccable craftsmanship to create evocative pieces that defy the distinctive categories of costume, couture and art. Also, her social activism saw her establish the first cybercafé in Senegal, the Metissacana, which

made the internet available to less-privileged people in parts of Dakar. She also founded the SIMOD, one of Dakar's premier fashion week events. Her works have featured prominently at the art biennial in Dakar and around the world, and featured on runways in the fashion capitals of New York, Milan, Paris and Johannesburg. Sy's costumes were featured in 'Making Africa: A Continent of Contemporary Design' produced in 2016 by the Guggenheim Museum Bilbao and the Vitra Design Museum, and in the 2021 exhibition 'Good as Gold' by Smithsonian's National Museum of African Art. Her designs are part of the permanent collection of the Museum of Black Civilizations in Dakar.

Chris Seydou

Known for his evocative creations in indigenous African textiles, notably, the Malian bogolanfini, Chris Seydou (1949-1994) was a pioneering African designer and an esteemed couturier. Born Seydou Nourou Doumbia, he began his illustrious journey in fashion as a tailor's apprentice in Kati, his hometown. He plied his trade between Kati and Ouagadougou before migrating further south to Abidjan, Côte d'Ivoire. While in Abidjan, he established an atelier and changed his name to Chris Seydou, in tribute to Christian Dior, whose work had greatly influenced his.

In 1972 Seydou moved to Paris, where he deepened his knowledge in haute couture, studying under luminaries such as Yves Saint Laurent and Paco Rabanne, both of whom became close acquaintances and collaborators later on in his career. Seydou's flair at merging Parisian couture with his African cultural sensibilities warmed the hearts of a rapidly expanding clientele base in Paris. His original take on European staples such as bustiers, bikers' jackets, bell-bottom trousers and miniskirts, rendered in indigenous African textiles made him an instant sensation.

In 1990, Seydou returned to Mali and established an atelier in Bamako. The designer could finally fulfil his dream of meeting the original makers of the bogolanfini, a textile that had constituted an important part of his practice in Europe. Seydou adopted the bogolanfini as his primary material, turning the famed couturier into a cultural agent and a catalyst for the development of the indigenous textile craft. When he began using the bogolan, Seydou was apprehensive about cutting the mysterious cloth. 'For me it was symbolic... I didn't want to cut bogolan early on; it was difficult to put my scissors to it'.[9] Furthermore, the irregular arrangement of the cloth's motifs and small width posed a technical challenge to the couturier. He addressed this by distilling or 'decoding' the most distinctive motifs for repetition and commissioning custom-woven cloths in adequate widths.

His experience at adapting the traditional cloth led to numerous collaborations. He worked particularly with textile manufacturers, such as the Industrie Textile du Mali, to produce factory-printed versions of the bogolanfini, greatly altering its form into an accessible textile that was more pliable to the needs of fashion and interior designers across the globe. Thanks to Seydou's creations the bogolan became, like kente, a familiar fulcrum of cultural identity for the African diaspora in the ever-expanding lexicon of fashionable African textiles. Seydou was also a founding partner of the Fédération Africaine de Createurs and served as its first president.

Alphadi

Hailed as the 'Magician of the Desert', Alphadi (b. 1957) has a Western couturier's flair infused with the culture and sartorial proclivities of the tribes of the Sahel Sahara. Born Sidahmed Seidnaly in Timbuktu, Alphadi trained at the Paris Atelier Chardon Savard school of fashion and design. He began his design journey under the tutelage of Yves Saint Laurent, Christian Lacroix and Paco Rabanne, and in 1985 launched 'Alphadi' at an international tourism show in Paris. Since then, Alphadi has showcased his works around the world, gracing catwalks in

New York, Tokyo, Milan, Paris, London, Johannesburg and in his home country, Niger. He works primarily with indigenous African textiles such as the Malian bogolanfini, the ndop, the khasa blankets of the Fulani, tie-dyed fabrics and wax prints. He elevates his works with embroidery and beading, incorporating subtle and surprising embellishments such as cowries and ostrich feathers.

Beyond his creative accomplishments, Alphadi has been astute in developing an expansive array of fashionable products and accessories. In 1999, he launched the sportswear line 'Alphadi Bis', and that same year he collaborated with Wrangler to produce Alphadi

Excerpts from the biennial FIMA fashion show held in Niamey, the capital of Niger.

Model walks the runway as creations by Sidhamed Alphadi are presented during the 2016 International Africa Fashion Festival in Agadez, Niger on December 17, 2016.

Jeans. In 2000, the designer created L'Air d'Alphadi, the first perfume ever created by an African designer. Alphadi works from his atelier in Niamey, Niger and retails his ready-to-wear

from mono stores in Paris and Abidjan. Alphadi is a founding member of the Fédération Africaine de Createurs (Federation of African Creators) and in 1998, he established the Festival International de la Mode (FIMA).

Alphadi chalked another phenomenal milestone in 2004, when he became the first African designer to showcase his works at the official haute couture season at the invitation of the Fédération de la Haute Couture et de la Mode (FHCM). And in 2016, he was designated as a UNESCO Artist for Peace in recognition of his commitment towards culture and development in the service of peace, respect and human dignity. For Alphadi, fashion is a tool for economic empowerment, fostering unity and encouraging the integration of Africa's diverse cultures into a single, indomitable force.

Pathé Ouedraogo

Pathé Ouedraogo (b. 1950) is another one of Africa's twentieth-century fashion legends. Throughout his illustrious career, the veteran designer has clothed distinguished personalities and political leaders, with former president Nelson Mandela of South Africa being his most cherished client. Maison Pathé'O is the unlikely story of a youngster that left his village in Burkina Faso in search of greener pastures in Abidjan, a bustling cosmopolitan city, which in

the 1980s held much allure for migrants in West Africa. His dream, quite modestly, was to forge a living in the foreign land and as proof of his success, return home with a bicycle and a radio.

With no formal knowledge of fashion, Ouedraogo mastered his newfound craft as a tailor's apprentice, improvising along the way with zeal and determination. In 1987, his hard work was recognized as he won the local 'Golden Scissors' award, but it was a decade later that he would get his biggest breakthrough. He credits the South African singer Miriam Makeba for purchasing his shirts as a gift for Nelson Mandela, who wore one on an official visit to France, causing much sensation and propelling him into the limelight. Pathé'O's creations have since graced the Moroccan King Mohammed VI, Rwanda's president Paul Kagame and Aliko Dangote, Africa's richest person.

Pathé'O prides itself in creating clothes that are either 100 percent or predominantly African, utilizing dyed textiles and wax print produced in the Ivory Coast. For Dior's 2020 Cruise collection, Pathé'O worked closely with Maria Grazia Chiuri to create look 58 in honour of the late Nelson Mandela. Impressed by Pathé'O's body of work and the distinct craftsmanship of Africa's material culture, Chiuri observed that 'true "Made in Africa" has always been luxury fashion'. Maison Pathé'O, now headquartered in the Cocody district of Abidjan, preserves the legacy of the distinguished designer, while promoting African fashion.

Art dress by Kofi Ansah, a composition of handwoven kente evening dress complete with headwrap and custom designed necklaces.

Kofi Ansah

Known as 'L'enfant terrible de la mode Africaine', Kofi Ansah (1951–2014) was one of Africa's pioneering designers and a revered figure in the Ghanaian fashion industry. Ansah began his journey as a designer in London after graduating from the Chelsea School of Art and Design. He got off to an impressive start in couture after making a gorgeous beaded gown for Princess Anne, and plied his trade in London dressing other distinguished personalities until his return to Ghana in 1992.

Back in Ghana, he set up an atelier under the name Artdress, an apt moniker for a designer who perceived himself more as an artist, a master craftsman who composed the most captivating silhouettes from indigenous textiles, jewellery and artforms. As an advocate of indigenous textiles, Ansah favoured materials including the kente, which he used sparingly for the most exclusive pieces, the bogolanfini, indigo-dyed fabrics and the imitation wax print, which he designed and commissioned especially for his exclusive use. He was famed for his precision and exacting approach to couture, employing techniques such as quilting and embroidery and unusual accessories such as the gourd, brass figurines and cowries. His collections were shown in New York, London, Paris, Milan and Rome and he received a standing ovation in 2009 at the Altaroma International Couture show in Rome, a prestigious biennial haute couture event.

Ansah advocated passionately for the development of the local textile and garment industry in Ghana and Africa. Emphasizing the need to unlock the potential of the commercial fashion industry for job and wealth creation, he stressed that 'We can't always hinge our industry on the exclusive, we need to tap into the commercial'. Although he served as president of the Federation of African designers, his greatest impact was on Ghana's own fashion industry, spearheading groundbreaking initiatives such as the National Friday Wear programme, which encouraged nationwide adoption of indigenous textiles and clothes on Fridays for the business sector. He also mentored many young protégés. When he passed away in 2014, he was accorded a stately burial by the government of Ghana.

Marianne Fassler

Leopard Frock by Marianne Fassler (b. 1949) is a story of distinguished craft, innovation and relentless enterprise, captured in a career that has spanned over forty years. Young Marianne would make clothes for herself and friends and was encouraged to take up private design and pattern-cutting classes while studying towards her honours degree in literature and the history of art at the University of Witwatersrand. In 1974, she showed her first collection, while still a student, and followed it up with a grander show in 1976, heralding her prolific career in fashion.

Fassler wields an unusual command on textures, dramatic prints and patterns; her most eclectic pieces project a playful and exuberant Africanism that avoids cliché. Her irreverence, inspired by unorthodox designers such as Zandra Rhodes, Ossie Clark and Japanese deconstructionists Yoji Yamamoto and Rei Kawakubo, frees her from the shackles of trends, instead anchoring the fashion house in values of craftsmanship, quality, ethics and flair.

Fassler's work evokes the diversity of African culture, incorporating indigenous

techniques such as layering, beadwork, and intricate embroidery. She also recycles and upcycles fabrics from previous seasons, employing patchwork and appliqué to invent inimitable pieces, placing sustainability at the heart of Leopard Frock. A champion of diversity and inclusivity, Fassler flexed the soft power of fashion in 1976 by sending a Black model down the runway in defiance of the apartheid regime. Besides this, the designer has chalked many firsts, such as opening a mono store in Hyde Park Corner, Johannesburg, and launching a perfume range. Labelled affectionately as the 'Queen of Frock' and the reigning doyenne of South African fashion, her pieces have shown at prestigious exhibitions internationally and at the Zeitz MOCAA in commemoration of the 21st anniversary of South African Fashion Week.

Beyond the Canon

Africa has seen many other illustrious designers, trailblazing both on the continent and abroad. These include Ghana's Tetteh Adzedu, an honoree of the 1998 Prince Claus Award, and Ugandan designer Sylvia Owori who designed the costume for *Last King of Scotland*. South Africa boasts couture sensation Peter Soldatos and deconstructionist Clive Rundle. In Nigeria, couture queen Deola Sagoe is renowned for her exacting take on aso-oke and luxurious lace fabric, while Lisa Foliwayo belongs to the vanguard of contemporary designers defying boundaries.

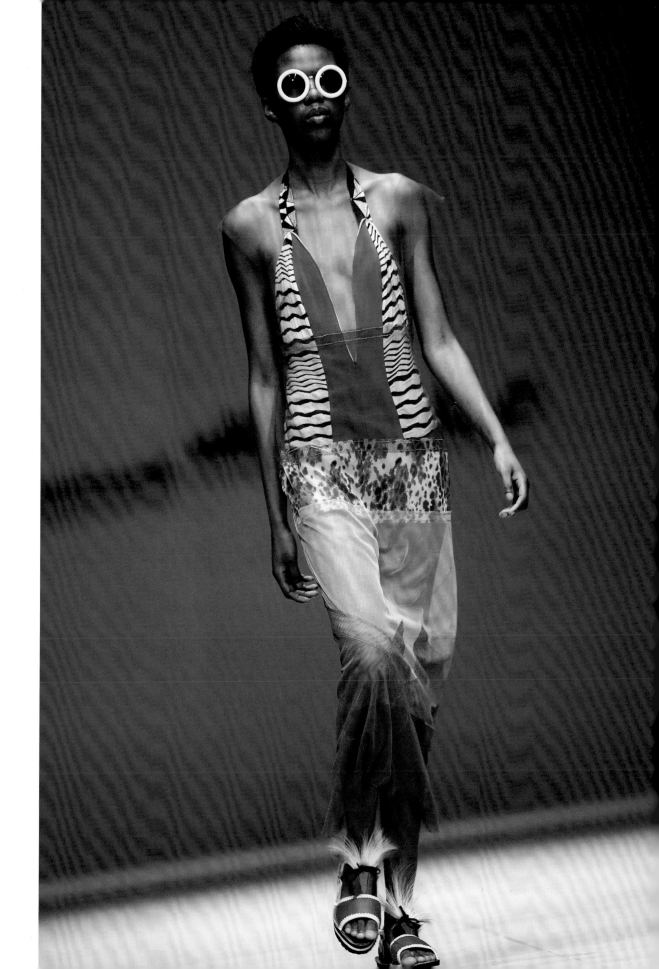

An Oasis of Luxury

Luxury encompasses the enduring tenets of rarity, craftsmanship, quality and culture. However, the definition of luxury as a universal phenomenon is elusive and subjective, depending on socio-economic and cultural contexts. For some, despite the success of the pioneering designers discussed above, the juxtaposing of Africa and luxury nevertheless evokes ambivalence. This impression is premised on the notion of a continent in despair[10] and the misconception of luxury as hegemonic to Europe. Yet luxury has existed since antiquity, manifesting in almost every culture with some form of social stratification, including those in Africa.[11] Indeed, besides manifesting luxury throughout the centuries of its evolving material culture, Africa's abundant natural resources have served as the bedrock to the development of the global luxury economy.

The Lotte Accra is Accra's prestigious address, established to house and promote a carefully curated selection of top luxury brands from the continent of Africa.

Opposite
The iconic Alara Lagos, purveyor of contemporary African luxury and lifestyle brands.

Beyond Europe, Africa was the fulcrum of trade in luxury goods to many parts of the globe (see pp. 14-19) and naturally, much of its prolific textile and craft heritage thrived as a result of the extensive trade in luxury goods. Through the dexterity of master craftspeople, and the distinctive taste of the nobility, rare and luxurious articles pervaded the lexicon of Africa's material culture for centuries. The discovery of the world's oldest jewellery, the 7,000-year-old Nassarius shell beads is an irrefutable testament of Africa's longstanding craft and luxury heritage (see p.52). And, of course, from the prestigious raphia cloth of the Tio (see p.172) to the kente produced exclusively for the courts of the Ashanti King (see p.38) many fineries and artefacts of remarkable beauty abound in the courts of Africa's mighty empires. Indeed, the dexterity and artistic ingenuity embodied in such profoundly beautiful objects continue to baffle the world,

including those most doubtful of Africa's enduring luxury heritage.

Luxury in contemporary Africa

A rapidly expanding market for luxury goods in leading economies such as South Africa, Nigeria, Egypt, Morocco and Mauritius has prompted the influx of numerous international brands in Africa. South Africa, the crown jewel of Africa's luxury-goods market has the biggest footprint of international brands nestled in retail hotspots such as Hyde Park Corner, Diamond Walk and the Mall of Africa. In Nigeria, Lagos and Abuja are also at the fore, with notable retailers including Temple Muse and Alara Lagos.

However, despite the potent combination of a steadily growing luxury-goods market, a rich cultural heritage, and the abundance of natural resources such as gold and diamonds,

Africa benefits marginally, if not insignificantly, as a source of luxury goods in the global economy. This paradox is underpinned by a multiplicity of challenges from the persistent impact of colonization in Africa, in which the potential for industrialization, and the development of indigenous craft industries were greatly impaired, to the inability or tacit disinterest of various African governments in harnessing the potential of culture and luxury for wealth creation and economic growth. In the contemporary context of luxury fashion, Africa's formidable industry is therefore relatively recent, evolving since the twentieth century under the patronage of pioneering designers, innovators and couturiers, who continue to negotiate Africa's role as a competitive site for the production of luxury.

African Markets

Africa entered the twenty-first century with renewed optimism based on a relatively stable economic and political landscape. Two decades later, and following the impact of the coronavirus pandemic, the excitement of a continent on the cusp of radical economic transformation has simmered down. Nevertheless, Africa's youthful population, rapid urbanization and the proliferation of technology continues to offer immense growth potential for diverse sectors of its economy, including fashion manufacturing and retail. An expanding middle class and the rising number of high-net-worth individuals is further impetus to growth in the luxury retail sector.

The potential of Africa's combined market for luxury goods, estimated at $6.1 billion in 2020 by Business of Fashion (BoF),[12] has attracted a bevy of global brands such as Dior, Gucci, Louis Vuitton, Versace, Giorgio Armani, Zegna, Chloé, Burberry, Hermès and Coach to luxury retail hotspots across the continent. For example, South Africa generated over US$15 billion in revenue from retail trade in textiles, clothing and footwear in 2019, with luxury goods accounting for US$4 billion of the total.[13] South Africa accounts for approximately a third of the total volume of luxury goods consumed in Sub-Saharan Africa in the same year. However, there has been a surge in the development of high-end retail infrastructure across the continent. For example, the total number of mega-malls in Africa, excluding South Africa, doubled between 2012 and 2020. The expanding retail infrastructure in Nigeria, Kenya, Egypt, Rwanda and Ghana just to name a few signals growth in Africa's formal retail economy.[14]

Amid the proliferation of mega-malls, there has also been a rise in niche boutique retail infrastructure. In Lagos, Alara serves as a creative hub for luxury and art. The iconic store, designed by David Adjaye celebrates African luxury through a carefully curated range of lifestyle brands across fashion, design and art. In South Africa, Merchants on Long and House of NALA stock Africa's leading luxury brands. Other notable boutiques include Temple Muse in Nigeria, the Lotte, and Viva Concept stores in Ghana. Furthermore, the use of technology to overcome infrastructure difficulties is unlocking greater value across the retail supply chain. Technology is bridging the gap in largely informal markets, enabling retailers and consumers to confront pressing challenges.

Industrial parks in Ethiopia for textile and garment manufacturing. The Eastern African economy has become a prominent hub for mass manufacturing of garment and shoes.

Employees of Stil Nua's fashion work at a textile factory in an industrial park connected to a free-trade zone in the Moroccan city of Tangiers on March 13, 2018.

E-commerce

The proliferation of internet-enabled smartphones, a youthful and digitally savvy population, coupled with improving digital payment solutions, is spurring growth in e-commerce in Africa. E-commerce in Africa, estimated at $20 billion in 2020, is dominated by a handful of disruptive players. Pioneer e-commerce retailer Jumia became the first African technology start-up to be listed on the New York Stock Exchange in 2019 while fashion retail platform Afrikrea raised US$1 million of the first round of investment capital in 2020.

In luxury e-retail, platforms such as Onchek, Ichuyu, Folklore and Industrie Africa are leveraging the power of e-commerce and storytelling to adequately position African brands in the global luxury market. African brands Kenneth Ize, Orange Culture, Casablanca and Tokyo James are also sold on brownsfashion.com, the luxury e-commerce arm of Farfetch. Furthermore, direct-to-market e-commerce stores and social-media platforms, such as Instagram, Facebook and WhatsApp offer remarkable flexibility to the retail operations of African brands.

In spite of the potential, e-commerce in Africa is still plagued by threats of cyber-fraud and the absence of adequate logistical and supply-chain infrastructure. While significant progress has been made, Africa could deepen its gains if the synergy between its e-commerce economy and bricks-and-mortar stores are adequately leveraged.

Potential as a manufacturing hub for luxury

Beyond the potential of consumer market, the continent is generating interest as a manufacturing hub for luxury. The 2012 edition of the *International Herald Tribune* Conference, which convened over 500 global leaders in luxury explored Africa's potential as a manufacturing hub for luxury goods. The event featured leading voices, such as Simone Cipriani from the Ethical Fashion Initiative (EFI, see below and p.79), who advocated for just trade – over aid – in Africa. Speaking at the fifth annual edition of the Condé Nast International Luxury conference held in Cape Town in 2019, editor of *Vogue International* and leading advocate of African fashion Suzy Menkes eulogized Africa as a global frontier of culture and craft. The event which was held under the theme 'The Nature of Luxury', greatly deepened the debate on Africa's emergent luxury market and its potential as a hub for the manufacture and retail of luxury.

A model walks the runway at the Edun Fashion Show during Mercedes-Benz Fashion Week, Fall 2015 at Skylight Modern on February 15, 2015 in the Brooklyn borough of New York City.

Opposite
Naomi Campbell graces the runway of Arise fashion show in Lagos, Nigeria. in 2020.

While African luxury gains ground, the legacy of certain failures and inefficiencies in indigenous textile and apparel industries continues to haunt the supply chain, with dire ramifications on the operations of many brands in Africa. In 2018, LVMH divested its interest in Edun, the first brand in LVMHs portfolio that was wholly produced in Africa. Suno, another promising brand that had a manufacturing footprint in Kenya shut its doors in 2016 after eight years of operation. While the closure of Edun and Suno resulted in part from divestiture and difficulties in acquiring investment capital, it underscores the precariousness of Africa's luxury industry. Indeed, sustaining a successful supply chain for luxury goods in Africa is a steep learning curve for many brands.

Funding persists as a bottleneck to the growth potential of indigenous African brands. Thankfully, recent developments indicate a favourable shift, with the emergence of industry specific investment vehicles such as Birimian. Other establishments such as the Fashion Agent in South Africa provide wholesaling, licensing and distribution services to a growing list of brands, while Africa Fashion Foundation (AFF), the Ethical Fashion Initiative (EFI) and the AfDB's Fashionomics are impacting the industry

through diverse forms of hands-on capacity building, upskilling and business development services. With the support of EFI brands such as Fendi, Stella McCartney, Vivienne Westwood have established supply chain operations in Africa. Furthermore, the tenacity of independent indigenous brands is most remarkable, AAKS, an ethical brand based in Kumasi sources handmade raffia bags in the northern region of Ghana against the odds for the global market. Tongoro Studio (see p.186) in Senegal is set on a mission to challenge stereotypes on 'Made in Africa'.

African luxury in the global media

In 2019, after headlining a sensational fashion show in Lagos, Naomi Campbell advanced calls for a Vogue Africa edition. This call illustrates the need for a cohesive voice to highlight creative talent on the continent.

Developments in the digital communication ecosystem from the 2010s to the 2020s, from Instagram and Facebook to TikTok, have guaranteed African brands' access to the global market. Print and digital media are

also important, with the most prominent print publications including *GQ South Africa*, *Wanted*, *Elle SA*, *Private Edition*, *Glitz Africa*, *BellaNaija Style* and *Genevieve* and the dominant digital media for fashion and lifestyle including *Nataal*, *Wanted Online*, *Jendaya*, *Afropolitain* magazine, *BellaNaija Style* and *Debonair Afrik*.

African fashion weeks are similarly crucial to showcasing African fashion to the world. Under the patronage of South African businesswoman and philanthropist Dr Precious Moloi-Motsepe, African Fashion International (AFI) is dedicated to unearthing and showcasing the best of African luxury to South Africa and the world. South Africa's premier fashion event, the South African Fashion Week (SAFW), has since the turn of the twenty-first century propelled many brands into the limelight. In West Africa, Arise Fashion Week founded in 2009 has evolved into a truly global platform, congregating not only leading names in African fashion but heavyweights from the African diaspora. Lagos Fashion Week is yet another trailblazer with a pan-African purview. Founded by entrepreneur and African fashion advocate Omoyemi Akerele, Lagos Fashion Week in partnership with its sister agency Style House Files provides a holistic platform for the development of African brands. Other distinguished runway events include the Glitz

Africa Fashion event, the Accra Fashion Week, the Dakar Fashion Week and, of course, the prestigious FIMA.

The year 2020, despite being perilous to economies around the world, witnessed one of the most intense media blizzards to hit African fashion. The power of pop culture swung fully behind Africa's creative economy, with blockbuster releases such as *Black is King* and *Coming 2 America*. *Black is King*, the 2020 visual album by Beyoncé inspired by Disney's 2019 screenplay *The Lion King*, leveraged the abundance of creative talent in Africa, featuring more than a dozen looks from designers such as Loza Maléombho, Adama Paris and Tongoro Studio. The kaleidoscope of fashion in 'Black is King' parallels the riveting afro-futuristic costumes that accompanied the 2018 blockbuster movie *Black Panther*. The 2021 movie *Coming 2 America*, which saw a cast arrayed in sumptuously embroidered kaftans, beaded costumes, knits and jewellry from leading African brands, sustains the momentum of African fashion in global media. In this period, Africa has also witnessed a wave of groundbreaking collaborations with reputable global brands. Dior's 2020 resort collection, for example, tapped into a wealth of design and creative talent from Africa by honouring the West African heritage of wax print through the lens of Ivorian designer Pathé'O (see p.71) and spotlighting the cause of a Moroccan-based craft collective, Sumano. An exciting list of collaborations followed suit, such as the Mantsho X H&M Kenneth Ize X Karl Lagerfeld, and the lemlem X H&M collaborations.

Sisters Of Afrika Collection
(Senegal Collective) during
AFI Fashion Week on
October 30, 2021 in
Johannesburg, South Africa.

Above
Beyoncé in Nguni 'Cow' leather print ensemble complete with braided hair and horn headdress. Beyoncé's visual album *Black is King* featured more than a dozen looks from notable African designers.

Left
Main cast of *Black Panther*, a fictional Wakanda that held fashion and movie lovers around the world spellbound. Costume designer Ruth E. Carter won an Oscar for her work on *Black Panther*.

Above
Dior Cruise 2020 collection honours the house's long-standing history with Marrakech. The collection embodied a broad collaboration with African models, designer Pathé'O and Uniwax, an imitation wax print company based in the Ivory Coast.

Right
The critically acclaimed and Oscar awardee costumier Ruth E. Carter staged a comeback with Ankara prints, embroidery and brass figurines in *Coming 2 America*, the sequel to the 1988 comedy, *Coming to America*.

Louis Vuitton Men SS22 collection 'Uniting Opposites' by Virgil Abloh celebrates the diverse origins fashion subcultures around the world.

The diaspora

In the global North, African and Black diasporic designers have made waves in the orthodox world of luxury. Architect and streetwear designer Virgil Abloh (1980–2021) took the reins as head of menswear at Louis Vuitton in 2018. A year before Abloh's remarkable feat, Ghanaian-born fashion editor Edward Enninful rose to become editor-in-chief of British *Vogue*, making him the first Black editor to head any of the publishing behemoth's editions. There is also a cohort of trailblazing designers whose works contribute immensely to propelling Africa's cultural renaissance across the globe. They including Joe Casely-Hayford, Ozwald Boateng, Duro Olowu, Adrien Sauvage, T-Michael of Norwegian Rain, Kerby Jean-Raymond, LaQuan Smith, Telfar Clemens and Dyenna Diaw of Peulh Vagabond. More than ever, diasporic designers are reconnecting to their African roots through collaborations with diverse indigenous African craft communities.

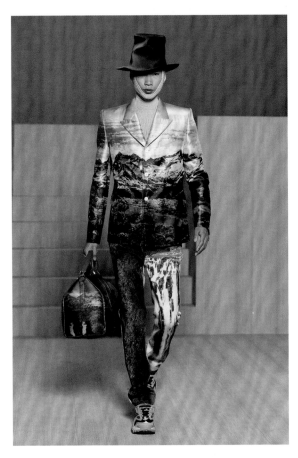

Luxe Ubuntu

Africa's emergence as a hub for luxury coincides with another highly significant phase in the evolution of the global industry. Over the past few decades many international luxury brands have come under criticism for unethical supply-chain practices and brazen infractions on human rights. The 2019 DW documentary, *Luxury: Behind the Mirror,* uncovered the disturbing reality of inhumane practices and exploitation, reinforcing the perception that behind the façade of glitzy advertising and marketing campaigns, lies a decaying industry.[15]

The twenty-first century luxury consumer is demanding more from brands, with sustainability, brand authenticity and value for handcraft becoming critical touchpoints for success. As the next frontier of luxury, Africa is uniquely positioned to turn the tide through sustainability and transparent value chain.

Introduced by Swaady Martin-Leke, founder of luxury tea brand Yswara, and academic Elizabeth Ellis,[16] Luxe Ubuntu is a philosophy that advocates for a new paradigm in which the successful luxury brand is underpinned by the African spirit of community and humanity. 'Ubuntu', which is carved from the Zulu proverb *Ubuntu ngumuntu ngabantu,*

Top
Luxury womenswear
designer LaQuan Smith
showcases his collection
at the 2021 New York
Fashion Week.

Bottom left
Fashion-Pyer Moss, New
York, United States, 10 July
2021. The latest fashion
from Pyer Moss is modeled,
in Irvington, NY. Staged at
the Villa Lewaro mansion,
the home built by African
American entrepreneur
Madam C.J. Walker in 1917.
The show was themed
around inventions by
African Americans.

Bottom right
Models present creations by
US designer Telfar Clemens
during the Paris Fashion
Week, in Paris, France,
23 September 2019. The
presentations of the SS
2020 Women's collections
run from 23 September to
2 October.

translates 'I am because you are' and is emblematic of the spirit of community and shared responsibility replete in many African cultures. Using the concept of Luxe Ubuntu as a basis, we can see Africa might lead the way in a global luxury reset by emphasizing the transformational vectors of culture, community, craftsmanship, sustainability and innovation.

Culture

Throughout the world, culture underpins the development of indigenous crafts and constitutes the lens through which luxury is explored and experienced. In Africa, particular values permeate the fabric of most indigenous cultures, with spirituality, empathy and humanity being the most familiar. In precolonial African societies, the extraction of resources for the production of crafts was approached with consideration to the environment. For example, the dye pits of Kofar Mata (p.45) which have existed for five centuries, maintain the use of natural dyes against the allure and convenience of readily available synthetic dyes. Similarly, Malian designer Aboubakar Fofana utilizes natural vegetable indigo dyes exclusively in a mission to revitalize and preserve the ancient craft of indigo dyeing in Mali. Such thoughtful considerations are underpinned by cultural values that prioritize the environment above financial profit. Other examples are replete in diverse forms of mindful consumption that characterize African cultures. Consequently, embedding African cultural values into the philosophy and supply chain practices of indigenous luxury brands can greatly impact the global luxury economy.

Improvisation is yet another trait of many

Print collection by Duro Olowu. The Nigerian-British designer is distinguished by his use of vivid prints and patterns. His silhouettes are structured and yet fluid, embodying a contemporary and timeless feel.

indigenous African cultures. Through resilience and adaptability, Africans have thrived whether they lived in abundance or scarcity. Through improvisation, objects, including waste, of both foreign and local origin have been transformed into objects of remarkable beauty and resourcefulness. This sensibility underpins the practices of many contemporary designers and artists who improvise, adapt, repurpose, upcycle and recycle an array of invaluable material and waste into distinctive products. A profusion of patterns, colours, techniques and objects, which are closely associated with improvisation are observed in the works of Duro Olowu, Marianne Fassler, Ituen Basi, Clive Rundle and ARTC. A cacophony of colours and patterns is an aesthetic greatly desired in many African cultures, as it could constitute a protective charm (akin to amulets) or signify the power, wealth and prestige of the wearer.[17]

Closely connected to culture is provenance, a reference to the source of manufacture of luxury goods, which deepens the bonds to indigenous cultures and authenticates the brand story. An excellent example of a brand that balances culture and provenance is Maxhosa, a wholly indigenous African brand that draws on the geometric patterns of intricate beadwork of the Xhosa people.

Community

Luxe Ubuntu as a paradigm of African luxury underscores the need for active collaborations, partnerships and continued engagements among brands and industry stakeholders. To every brand, the starting point of community is the value chain of craftsmen and consumers that falls under their immediate influence. Community encompasses the society to which the enterprise operates and the broader ecosystem of industry stakeholders. A deep level of consideration for community is the starting point of a harmonious balance between the internal operation and external networks of the brand.

Globally, the niche luxury sector is governed and nurtured under the auspices of reputable organizations such as the Walpole (UK), the

Fondazione Altagamma (Italy) and the Comité Colbert of France. While these establishments operate under the patronage of European governments, Africa is yet to possess a body with oversight responsibility over the development of its luxury industry. The South African Luxury Association (SALA), established in 2009 to convene and nurture the region's luxury and premium lifestyle sectors, may well be the first institution with such a mandate. In the spirit of community, Africa stands to benefit immensely by establishing similar organizations to foster collaboration and partnerships towards collective goals at the regional and pan-African levels.

Craftsmanship

Craftsmanship, the skill and dexterity of an artisan, is the single most enduring tenet of luxury. Throughout this volume, we explore the captivating works of spinners, weavers, dyers, embroiderers and others who have created objects of remarkable craftsmanship. African master artisans have exhibited rare proficiency in special processes from the proficiency in the lost wax technique as well as intricate handweaving and embroidery (see p.38).

In recent years, there has been renewed interest in products that are handcrafted due partly to consumers' desire for products imbued with the human touch and a sense of performance rather than the uniformity of industrial products. However, handcrafting, while a crucial factor in the paradigm of Luxe Ubuntu, is not enough to sustain luxury, particularly if artisanal skillsets are not adequately developed or aligned to the production of luxury goods. A lack of attention to the development of textile crafts in many regions of the continent has led to the declining quality in handcraft for many previously prestigious textiles. In a sad anecdote that illustrates this point, a master kente weaver after closely examining a woven kente cloth from the local market, shook his head in disapproval, bemoaning the inexperience and lack of ingenuity of contemporary weavers.[18]

In light of a resurgent interest in indigenous African textiles, it is imperative that African governments invest in the research and development of craft to forge unique competencies as a competitive advantage in the global luxury industry. A positive case in point is the Casa Moda Academy in Morocco, set up through the collaborative efforts of the Moroccan Association of Textile and Apparel Industries (AMITH) and the Moroccan government. Casa Moda draws on the expertise of local and international resources towards the development of the textile and apparel industries. This initiative is an excellent blueprint for public and private collaboration in the development of local textile industries.

Sustainability

Sustainability is defined as the ability of the present generation to fulfil their needs without compromising the ability of future generations to achieve the same. Sustainability underscores the relevance of conservation and consideration of the ecology while consuming.[19] The fashion industry is one of the largest polluters in the world, with luxury's association with excess and profligacy placing it further at odds with sustainability. Nevertheless, sustainability has become a critical determinant of success in the marketplace as consumers, supply-chain actors

and investors continue to scrutinize the supply-chain practices of brands.

As Africa's role in the global fashion supply chain evolves, the threats of unsustainable practices cannot be ignored. A 2019 report by NYU-Stern found that factory workers earned an appallingly low wage of $26 per month in a factory in Ethiopia, while another report in 2021 by Water Witness International cited threats to livelihoods resulting from the pollution of rivers and water bodies by industrial clothing manufacturers in Lesotho and Tanzania. Clearly, tapping the potential of the textile and apparel industries for economic growth is a delicate quest requiring greater caution.

Fortunately, Africa is already blazing the trail in sustainable sourcing, with organizations such as the EFI facilitating access to ethically manufactured luxury goods for reputable brands around the world. Africa's sustainable praxis is most profound in the luxury goods sector as artisans rank among some of the highest paid in the world. AAKS, an independent luxury brand in Ghana sees luxury as a tool for social good and operates a supply chain that empowers women weavers in the

Star tulle dress with embroidered corset composed of poly blend and cotton; Christie Brown.

From 'Heritage meets the classics' – AW 21 collection fuses a variety of materials, techniques and silhouettes to reinterpret the classic look. It is accentuated with iconic stools by Tekura.

northern region of Ghana. In 2018, AAKS and the UNHCR launched Weaving for Change, which provided new skills and access to fair and dignified work for displaced women seeking refuge in Burkina Faso. Another excellent example is Brother Vellies, an ethical shoe brand that prides itself in a supply chain and labour practice that is wholly sustainable.

Africa is also leading the charge in setting sustainable standards in the operations of industries involved in the supply of raw materials. In South Africa, where 50 percent of the mohair employed in the global luxury industry is sourced, Mohair South Africa oversees the strict adherence to ethical and sustainable practices among its members,

building synergies between Angora goat farmers, fashion designers and research institutions. In the world of gemstones, Africa spearheaded the establishment of the Kimberly Process to stem the trade in conflict diamonds, ensuring that diamonds traded on the global exchange were not catalysts to conflict in regions such as the Democratic Republic of Congo and Angola. Through many similar country and regional initiatives, Africa is continually delivering on the promise of sustainability and in the process laying the foundation for an ecologically friendly luxury supply chain.

Opposite

AAKS and UNHCR Weaving for Change provides skill training and a livelihood for refugees from Sudan. The range of products include lamps and a wide assortment of homeware.

Below

The Torero backpack in purple and aqua. The 'Wear it for a Cause' collection epitomizes the definition of luxury and sustainability, experimenting with unconventional materials, cut and bold colours. The collection is made with Reform studio's eco-friendly signature material 'Plastex' and high-end genuine leather.

Innovation

Technological and managerial innovation are crucial pathways to success in the highly competitive global luxury industry. Fundamental to fashion's innovative future are systems for retail management including artificial intelligence (AI), augmented reality (AR), big data, and revolutionary infrastructure for production such as 3D printing and other forms of fully automated garment-manufacturing systems. In recent times, new innovations are emerging at the intersection of couture and gaming, with the explosive trend of digital clothing for personal avatars in the form of non-fungible tokens (NFTs) making the waves. In Africa, where brands operate under

extremely difficult environments, innovation fundamentally guarantees efficiency, productivity and growth, while providing a pathway for leadership. Furthermore, the chronic existential challenges to manufacturing, distribution and retail, as well as the impact of the global coronavirus pandemic, may well provide the right impetus for brands to innovate.

In the absence of a dedicated and globally oriented industry magazine for African fashion, many African brands have, through the power of social media, succeeded in creating new narratives. Similarly, in retail, the absence of adequate physical retail infrastructure has fostered a budding generation of indigenous e-retail and commerce platforms. Digital fashion has also seen early adopters such as the eclectic virtual shows by Hannifah, and Tongoro Studio.

Throughout Africa there are examples of brands that leverage innovation and emergent technologies to leapfrog challenges. Other remarkable examples include, from Thebe Magugu (see p.126), a trench coat collection, produced with proprietary anti-viral fabrics that are capable of killing 99 percent of viruses and bacteria that come in contact with its surface. This ingenuity constitutes a pioneering breakthrough in the global field of anti-viral textiles. The Kenneth Ize Loom, designed to enhance efficiency and productivity of indigenous West African weavers constitutes another noteworthy feat. The loom, which was developed with support from the Impact Fund for African Creatives (IFFAC) also underscores the importance of venture capital support for research and development in Africa's creative economy.

Luxury industry of the future

As markets shift and values are realigned, the orthodox world of luxury is being disrupted. The very meaning of luxury is in flux, manifesting in novel forms, product categories and experiences across disparate regions of the world. In the context of extensive trade and cultural exchange, Africa's indigenous textile and apparel industries have evolved, bringing to light a venerable and dynamic luxury heritage.

Today, Africa is basking in the most potent cultural and creative renaissance, which has culminated from decades of economic and creative transformation. The potential of African markets, the global reputation of its designers, and the abundance of valuable natural resources and handcrafting skills offer a real opportunity to build a buoyant fashion manufacturing industry with a high-value and luxury craft sector atop the pyramid. Governments and industry stakeholders need to explore effective strategies that capitalize on this opportunity. The development of Africa's indigenous textile and apparel industry can only thrive if it incorporates the ideals of Luxe Ubuntu and emphasizes the role of institutions with educational and oversight mandates. With the right framework, Africa is poised to produce global brands that are anchored in the tenets of Luxe Ubuntu, ensuring the holistic wellbeing of the production ecosystem, the environment and consumers the world over.

Statement neckpiece and earring set from Jiamini's Mung'ung'uti ('Spine') collection. Form and fluidity, key tenets of the brand are replete in its luxurious and distinctive pieces.

New Wave of African Talent

African fashion, once cast to the periphery of the global economy, has, since the turn of the twenty-first century, undergone a seismic shift. Eclectic and nuanced, the contemporary African fashion scene is dynamic and in constant flux. In the previous chapter, we established the potential of Africa's fledgling luxury-goods industry, while enumerating its challenges. Despite these, a new wave of contemporary designers are charting new frontiers and courting the attention of global media. They are adept at preserving and promoting indigenous African cultures, accomplished through excellent craftsmanship and quality standards that resonate with luxury consumers around the world. The expansive list of creative talent includes the designers featured in the designer gallery (pp. 96-113) and case studies that compose this chapter, as well as many others whose innovative take on indigenous textiles, artforms, materials and aesthetics have captivated the world. Their success is predicated also on their savviness at adapting indigenous materials and textiles into commercially viable global luxury goods.

What follows is a careful selection of brands that reflect the diversity that exists in contemporary African luxury fashion – a diversity that encompasses both modern and traditional practices and production techniques, as well as gender, geography, culture and heritage. Exploring the worldview of these brands gives us an insight not only into the challenges they face, but also their ethos and ethics. It is a celebration of the very best of what Africa has to offer.

Designer Gallery

Imbokodo campaign by MmusoMaxwell. 'Imbokodo' is a Zulu word for stone. It is used allegorically for the courage of South African women in the face of adversity, from the oppression of the apartheid regime, to continued gender inequality and gender-based violence. (See MmusoMaxwell caption p.103.)

Opposite

Embroidered Bubu Dress by Adama Paris. Adama Paris caters to the modern and elegant woman, for whom the greatest luxury is to make things her own. The brand's line reflects this to-and-fro journey, this sharing between the West and Africa. Pieces from the collection include organic cotton handwoven and dexterously embroidered by Senegalese artisans.

Right

The Tigrette: feather collar trimmed with antique brass from the Tuareg Tribe by Kapoeta by Ambica. Kapoeta is an eco-brand that upcycles feathers and other materials, both organic and inorganic, preciousand semi-precious, into sensuous jewellery. The brand also employs captivating visuals and unconventional materials to contest the conventions of beauty and luxury.

Left

Tulle Bikini set with hand-fringed wool detailing from the SS21 collection 'Land of Gods' by I.AM. ISIGO. Shuffling between Lagos, Nairobi and Accra, designer Bubu OgIsi of I. AM.ISIGO embodies the energy of an itinerant creative. Through the ancient craft techniques of dyeing and weaving, the brand reinterprets the relationship between materials, craftsmanship, culture and spirituality. It remains at the forefront of the global slow fashion movement, curating and releasing a collection annually against industry conventions.

Opposite

Rebel Fanny and Belt bags by Reform Studio. The collection is produced from Plastex, a proprietary ecofriendly textile made with recycled plastic bags and polyester threads. The recyclable Plastex yarns are woven using traditional Egyptian weaving looms purposely to preserve the ancient technique and the livelihood of local craftspeople.

Opposite
Toni Africa coat from
SS 2020 by MmusoMaxwell.
MmusoMaxwell, founded
by Maxwell Boko and Mmuso
Potsane, is a ready-to-wear
womenswear brand. It
creates ethical garments
inspired by African heritage
and contemporary culture
with a particular emphasis
on tailoring: structure,
fit and detail. According
to the duo, the brand's
African heritage permeates
through the time-honoured
craftsmanship echoing that
of the ancient craftspeople.

Right
Chiffon-print shirt from the
Exclusive Pieces collection
by Allëdjo. 'Allëdjo', which
means 'travellers' in Yoruba
is curated for travel and
leisure, with each collection
dedicated to a destination
and its culture. The brand
seeks to create ethically
and with utmost regard
to indigenous cultural
values, while highlighting
the apparent simplicity
of complex designs.

RIght
Bead-encrusted and couture- finished bridal gown from the Nuptials collection by Pistis. Since 2008, Pistis has spearheaded the evolution of bespoke costumes and bridal gowns in Africa.

Opposite
Dual-tone leather and exotic skin bag from Zashadu. The piece from the Hero collection is made from sustainably-sourced crocodile skin and indigenous-sourced leather, which are dyed and hand glazed. The Hero collection 'was born out of a time of great darkness in my life' says designer Zainab Ashadu.

Opposite
Voluminous crinkle blouse
and wide leg jumpsuit with
corset by Christie Brown
SS20. Crinkle fabric and
polyester jersey is trimmed
with imitation wax print.
Founded in 2008, Christie
Brown celebrates the rich
culture and textile heritage
of Ghana, distilling the bold
West African aesthetic to
create riveting pieces and
edgy silhouettes that
resonate with modern
women the world over.

Right
The Hana Mini Blue from
Season 5 collection by
AAKS. Duotone woven
raffia with leather detailing.
AAKS handwoven raffia
bags are sourced and
manufactured in the
northern region of Ghana.
Each piece is made by
highly skilled master
craftswomen, who
painstakingly craft with
dexterity and intimate
knowledge of the local
raffia yarns.

Left

The Tiered Trio: The Rudo, Alizeti and Lune maxi dresses from the Christine Collection by Sika'a. Sika'a is a contemporary womenswear luxury brand inspired by the beauty, tradition and culture of Africa. The brand combines textures, colours and patterns to celebrate and elevate the African form. Sika'a pieces are bold, vibrant and designed to be versatile in use.

Opposite

Masii clutch bag, and Yatta earrings from the Mung'ung'uti collection by Jiamini. The clutch is composed of handwoven sisal and wool, with white pearl and black bead detailing. The earrings are intricately woven from glass seed beads attached to vertebrae cast from 18k gold-plated brass. The Mung'ung'uti (meaning 'spine') collection is inspired by the vast system network of pathways that connect the succession of generations. The processes employed encapsulate the three core founding principles of Kenyan-based luxury brand Jiamini: tradition, craftsmanship and heritage.

Previous
The Veterans Pursuit AW collection by David Tlale. Revered for his impeccable execution of style, cut and fit David Tlale is the epitome of luxury. The Veterans Pursuit collection is inspired by military might, symbolizing the brand's dauntless journey and pieces are influenced by the Victorian era. Models wear the brand's signature- print dress, camo logo print Yeoman Coat and a harmond satin camo logo print shirt layered under the Abner Jacket.

Left
Cantadora Earings - Keeper of stories from SS 2021 Nascent Collection by Pichulik. The name 'Cantadora' is drawn from Spanish folklore, meaning 'one who passes down myths and stories by word of mouth'. The earrings are composed of curved brass looped with soft hemp rope detail and finished with a titanium pin. The collection celebrates the regenerative forces of rebirth.

Opposite
Vasco unisex wool felt hat by Simon and Mary. Known for its contemporary twist on the military Fez, Simon and Mary adapts its uncommon expertise and a heritage of hat making to produce pieces of exceptional finishes, colourways and materials. Established in 1935 by Mordechai Pozniak, Simon and Mary has witnessed a contemporary rejuvenation under the creative direction of Mordechai's grandson Dean Pozniak, establishing it as one of Africa's few trans-generational brands.

Lukhanyo Mdingi

Cape Town-based designer and winner of the coveted Karl Lagerfeld Award at the 2021 LVMH Prize, Lukhanyo Mdingi founded his eponymous brand in 2015. The brand embodies Mdingi's unrelenting desire to create with intent and soulfulness, which is manifested through the meticulous and time-honoured techniques of weaving, knitting, and appliqué to a visual feast of unconventional textures. He considers time as a crucial element of luxury, and speaks of 'using the spirit of time in the best way, in order to create quality items'. The brand, according to the designer is constantly evolving, embracing the concept of collaboration in its present phase of evolution. Collaborating with an illustrious list of designers and craft communities around the continent accords Mdingi the opportunity to explore indigenous materials, textures and artforms to create sophisticated and elegant pieces such as the Coutts Collection, which honours the legacy of textile artist and designer

Nicholas Coutts. Through collaboration, Mdingi celebrates the distinctive skills and exceptional craftsmanship of indigenous craft communities and individuals in Africa. The brand has shown in New York, Cape Town and at the Pitti Immagine: Generation Africa Stage. The pieces by Mdingi are composed of premium raw material and textiles, many of which are indigenous to South Africa. They include angora kid mohair, merino wool and silk.

What inspired the establishment of your brand?

When I first started the label, I was driven by the desire to create pieces that were timelessly elegant. My mission was to bridge the gap between artisanal craft and modern designs. However, as time went by, I came to the realization that there are many hands involved in the value chain of the brand, and that the entire value chain was about relationships. This

Previous
COUTTS handwoven scarf from the Lukhanyo Mdingi X
Nicholas Coutts collection. An ode to mastery, the scarf
is a hybrid of mixed medium yarns, with an inimitable
hyper-textured result. The scarf is paired with the
Lukhanyo Mdingi hand-felted Kid Mohair and Merino
wool fisherman jacket.

Opposite
Pieces from Perennial AW19 collection. Perennial represents
a mindful approach to design development and a focus
on timeless essentials. The collection is also characterized
by its choice of delicate and luxuriant material mediums,
including pure Angora kid mohair and merino wool. Top
left and right: ivory turtle-neck shawl made from knit
Angora Kid Mohair and layered under-brushed merino-wool
bomber jacket. In the same frame model wears a Silk blend
Heneke Manderin shirt-jacket and pants. Bottom left and
right: ivory Heneke Trench composed of brushed Angora
kid mohair and pure merino wool blend.

was the moment where I began to envision the
brand as a springboard by which every one of
these individuals could reach their potential.
This new realization has also made me sensitive
to the power of collaborations, where a certain
kind of honesty and humanness is manifested.
The brand now revolves around the concept of
collaboration, where the very opportunity to
work with diverse craft communities offers us
the ability to create something more than design
– a manifestation of ingenuity, honesty and a
mindful consideration for what we do.

How does culture influence your design practice?

Culture is a critical dimension of Lukanyo Mdingi,
more so in the context of collaboration, where
distinctive cultures often intersect. We are, for

example, working with a Kenyan brand called
Jermini in a project that provides us the avenue to
bridge artisanal craft and modernity but most
importantly, highlights the values in our distinctive
cultures. Through this collaboration, there is
some form of cultural exchange, in which the
rich cultural heritage observed in the peculiar
way of their traditional tapestry and weaving of
the sisal plant is imparted to the brand. Their
story within our label is really special, offering
us the unique opportunity to partake in a
culture that would ordinarily be alien to us.

You work primarily with indigenous textiles and materials. What is the motivation behind this?

Sourcing in Africa is not an easy task, but it means
we have to be incredibly resourceful in our choice
of textiles and we try to utilize to the best of our
abilities what is at our disposal. Because the
reality is we don't have access to the fabrics
and textiles we see on the runways and that are
available to our counterparts in other parts of
the world. However, this limitation has also
become the compelling reason for us to work
hand in hand with local artisans to develop
indigenous textiles. Through the motions, we
have become sensitive to the evocative art of
handcrafting and its visually striking and tactile
outcomes. There is, I must say, an obsession
with craft and how it can be transformed
through modern design in a sublime and
seamless way. Our longest collaboration is with
Stephanie Bentum, creator of handmade, felted
textiles for both fashion and interiors, whose
primary medium is mohair and merino wool.
Her practice evokes these tenets that I say have
become essential to the brand, the sense of

humanness, honesty and the dexterity only possible to the human hands, and I think if we are in the position to immerse ourselves in such a praxis then that is exactly what we will do.

What do you consider as luxury?

I think luxury is subjective; it has to do with circumstances, conditioning, education and who you are and what you think. I grew up thinking Woolworths was luxury, but with the exposure that I have right now, that is no longer the paradigm. So, luxury is quite relative, and almost impossible to pigeonhole. Depending on the socio-economic and cultural context, luxury can be anything and everything at the same time. However, personally, I think luxury is when we are able to create with a sense of consideration, mindfulness and time, and also the use of the human hand, I think that is the ultimate luxury. More so as a designer, working with human beings and feeling their spirit and relishing the pieces that we are able to create together.

Is there such a thing as African luxury?

Generally, luxury is a universal phenomenon, one that is difficult to pigeonhole, and which makes geographical categorization just as elusive. However, I also think the designer's origin and their ethos can contribute to such categorization. For example, I am African, so I am naturally inclined to draw on my African heritage or exhibit some aesthetic influence from the African culture. But then again, my exception to the compartmentalization of luxury based on geography is how they easily crumble in the context of a rapidly globalizing world. For example, how would my brand be categorized if I relocated to Australia and produced in that

Opposite
Pieces from Perennial AW19 by Lukhanyo Mdingi. Main image: Zimmermann dress in spiced tobacco, composed of Angora kid mohair and pure merino wool blend. Top right: jacket composed of Angora kid mohair and pure Angora blend. Brushed merino wool jumper and pants.

country? Would it be 'Australian' luxury? Nevertheless, as a person that values collaboration, I believe that if there ever was such a thing as African luxury, it will be an embodiment of community and craftsmanship.

You place a premium on Africa's textile heritage. Do you believe that Africa can establish a competitive advantage in the global luxury economy by harnessing the uniqueness of indigenous textiles?

Yes, I am mindful about prioritizing the use of indigenous textiles in my work. We are disadvantaged in terms of production infrastructure, as very few facilities exist on the continent with the capacity to produce quality that meets international standards. However, when it comes to textiles, I believe we do have the ultimate in luxury. Unfortunately, we have not capitalized on the unique expertise evident in the vast array of textile cultures in Africa, with these industries seeing little to no support from governments. In the absence of such support and infrastructure, a collaborative spirit is the ideal means by which Africa can assert its place in the global luxury economy.

Adele Dejak

In many East African cultures, jewellery conveys status and embodies a deep symbolism. Unsurprisingly, this region prides itself in a profound jewellery heritage, including the intricately beaded necklaces of the Maasai in Kenya and the ornate ancient jewellery and Coptic crosses of Ethiopia. Adele Dejak is an accessible luxury brand that epitomizes African craftsmanship, culture, sustainability and empowerment. At Adele Dejak, the fiery furnace by which each piece is created is allegorical of the journey of the bold and fearless 'modern warrior'. At the same time, the brand encapsulates the sophistication, elegance and vulnerabilities of contemporary women.

Undoubtedly one of Africa's jewellery powerhouses, Adele Dejak's journey into jewellery craft marks an improbable leap from a qualification in law to design. However, growing up in the Kano region of Nigeria, the designer recalls her fascination with the bold, evocative colours of indigenous African textiles and the intricate beadwork of the Hausa. With her memories equally imprinted with the eccentric adornment of the Fulani and Tuareg women, Dejak has established a unique aesthetic through her edgy, chunky and armour-like handmade statement pieces. Her jewellery and range of handbags are composed of readily available materials such as cow horns, cowhide, brass, and imitation wax print. Dejak counts Malian photographer Seydou Keïta, Italian visual artist Alberto Burri and British-Iraqi Architect Zaha Hadid as influences. Adele Dejak belongs to the prestigious Design Network Africa, a collective of accomplished designers of diverse backgrounds from East, West and Southern Africa.

Opposite
Falashina earrings and assorted rings by Adele Dejak. The Falashina, composed of upcycled brass is shaped like the gourd, it is symmetrical and creates a reflective illusion.

What is the guiding philosophy of Adele Dejak and how does it impact your product and the supply chain?

The guiding philosophy of Adele Dejak is quality craftsmanship, empowerment and sustainability. I take pride in the quality of my pieces and put sustainability at the forefront, the brand's mindful approach to production thrives at the point where indigenous knowledge, craftsmanship and locally sourced materials intersect. Furthermore, my works are influenced immensely by my African heritage and the materials in my immediate surroundings. It is paramount to honour our ancestors by preserving the gifts and skills they bestowed on us, my responsibility as a designer includes identifying and harnessing indigenous craftsmanship. All my pieces are handcrafted by skilled craftsmen in Kenya, and most of my jewellery pieces are sustainably made of recycled brass and aluminium, Ankole cow horn, Maasai and West African beads. For the handbag line, I use cowhide, Kuba cloth and African wax print. Adele Dejak is also about

empowerment in diverse ways, but most fundamentally, of our craftsmen, who receive the best training, and of our clients. As a brand, AD epitomizes sophistication, style and quality. Many pieces are bold for the 'modern warrior woman' as its important to empower women (and men) by body adornment.

How do you navigate the difficult terrains of sourcing in Africa and selling to global markets?

The growth of e-commerce has created a unique opportunity for African luxury brands to access international markets. Sourcing has always been a challenge as well as access to international markets. Unfortunately, there is a misconception about African brands that because we are African, we must be selling cheap curios! It can get frustrating dealing with potential clients who automatically assume this. They have no qualms spending hundreds of dollars on a European brand that's made with the same materials but are reluctant to spend on affordable handmade luxury. The brand has tried to change this narrative through good-quality photography and presentations on social media and look books. Social media has been of great help in navigating our way in the highly competitive fashion jewellery world.

What is luxury?

Luxury and the concept of luxury is changing fast. In my opinion, luxury is telling a story, a story that is anchored in humanity and relevant to one's own identity. It is a feeling, the joy of owning something that is handmade or just aesthetically pleasing. It is uniqueness, exclusivity in design and quality. It's the creation of personalized and fascinating experiences. It is timeless and has nothing to do with wealth or social status. The new luxury is actually sustainable, ethical and recycled, thus challenging traditional concepts of luxury. Luxury shapes cultures and African luxury is making its mark in the luxury market.

Is there such a thing as African luxury? and what makes luxury in Africa different?

Historically, Africa has always had a thriving luxury market. The wealthy and noble classes of ancient Africa enjoyed the beauty of luxurious and uniquely made products. Today, more people can access and afford luxury lifestyles and that's where we come in – by offering affordable luxury. What makes luxury in Africa different is that it is anchored in peculiar ancient traditions and values. Consequently, many of the contemporary brands of African origin embody these values, thereby creating an experience of luxury that is uniquely African.

How should Africa assert its place in the global luxury economy?

Africa has the world's second-fastest growing economy in the world. For centuries Africa has been a huge source of inspiration for artists and designers alike. African-inspired designs have already proven to be a huge hit in European markets. There is an existing gap that only African designers can fill. However, this cannot happen in a vacuum. We need to form strategic partnerships in both the public and private sectors to ensure fashion designers get access to resources such as capital and training to help them thrive in the competitive global market.

Below
The Ayoka statement neckpiece from the AMI collection produced with Lagos-based Afrominima Studios.

Opposite
The Dhamani Maureen neckpiece by Adele Dejak. This neckpiece consists of eight brass wires shaped into loops that are polished to a glow. The flow and rhythm of this statement piece is a testament to the dexterity indigenous Senegalese metalsmiths.

Thebe Magugu

Spy cameras and microphones printed inconspicuously onto garments, polka-dot dresses with finger print patterns and audio polygraphs, Thebe Magugu distils the SS21 collection of his eponymous brand through the captivating story of self-confessed spy Olivia Anne Marie Forsyth. In 'Alchemy' the AW21 collection, Magugu explores African spirituality, utilizing textures, colour hues and motifs to convey the crypted divination by stylist and real-life 'Sangoma' Noentla Khumalo. Such is the inventiveness of Magugu and his mastery in fashion and storytelling. He exudes a rare form of creativity and attuned sensibility that is grounded in African culture and yet atypical. Through authentic stories, excellent craftsmanship and distinctive silhouettes, he seeks to re-orient mindsets on South Africa's socio-political and creative economy. He launched an annual magazine called *Faculty Press*, a platform that elevates alternative voices across South Africa's vibrant creative economy.

Magugu's journey in fashion has been an eventful one. In 2019 his installation at the International Fashion Showcase (IFS) in London titled 'Dawning' won the top prize. He also clinched the LVMH prize that same year, becoming the first African designer to do so. These achievements have thrust him into the limelight with headliner editorials in *Vogue, Elle, Paper, I-D* and *Dazed* just to name a few. The Metropolitan Museum of Art in New York also acquired a Thebe Magugu dress for permanent display at the Costume Institute.

What is distinctive about the Thebe Magugu brand?

Education is the cornerstone of the brand, and something I hope to achieve through research

Opposite
Jacquard floral bomber with lilac tinsel dress from the Art History SS19 collection by Thebe Magugu.

and storytelling. I hold the conviction that fashion, contrary to widespread perceptions is deeply intellectual, and so I approach it inventively, constantly interrogating seemingly trivial aspects of the design process. Beyond the motions of my craft, my reverence for education is evident in my seasonal collections, which are named after university subjects. I took the idea of education further by starting *Faculty Press*, an annual zine that profiles, ideas, people and key moments within South African fashion and the wider creative economy. That notwithstanding, as a designer that values functionality and playful aesthetics, my products end up being the most fun and comfortable pieces.

How has Africa's cultural heritage shaped your work?

Africa has a rich cultural heritage that has, for decades, captured the imagination of the world. It is refreshing to see how the younger generation of African designers are reinterpreting this heritage through a globalized worldview, the result is something inimitable. Culture has a special place in my design practice, but I approach it unconventionally by dissecting popular narratives to uncover deeply embedded nuances that are at once historical and relevant to contemporary times. I think it is important to draw on Africa's heritage in a manner that preserves and projects it in the modern world. But apart from the idyllic, my work also confronts the irreverent aspects of culture that underpin social ills such as gender-based violence, racism and discrimination against people of different sexual orientation. Clothing is the medium through which I engage with the issues that are close to my heart, close to what is happening and close to my country.

Given the quality of craftsmanship in your work, how have you navigated the challenges of sourcing locally?

Given the exacting demands of the global luxury market and the standards of my brand, sourcing locally is anything but an idle walk in the park. South Africa and many other parts of the continent lack adequate infrastructure and skillsets suitable for producing luxury. At my pace of growth many assume I would just move production to Europe because it would be easier, but how could I lament the brain drain in my country and yet perpetuate the perception that that the best is somewhere out there in Europe? I do not intend to relocate irrespective of the challenges. The Covid-19 pandemic has underscored the need to develop a robust local supply chain and, consequently, deepened my resolve to contribute to building local competencies. I am pleased thus far with the output of the artisans and master craftpeople in my network, the exceptional quality and product finish speaks to the potential of Africa's niche luxury sector.

In light of your recent breakthrough in the development of anti-viral textile technology, in what ways can innovation propel Africa's luxury industry?

I think the continued uptake and investment in technologies across production and design will continue to move Africa's trajectory further and higher. The talent, creativity and work ethic is there; this just needs to be galvanized through innovation and technology to foster the establishment of a viable industry. To clarify on investment, I think it should be one that is mutually beneficial. There is a trend now

Right
Printed dress comprising a repeat motif of fingerprints from the SS21 collection, Counter Intelligence by Thebe Magugu. The dress is complemented by a mustard military fez, emblazoned with Thebe Magugu sisterhood emblem. The fingerprint belongs to confessed South African spy Olivia Anne Marie Forsyth (Agent No. RS407, Code name 'Lara'), who was planted undercover at Rhodes University as a student from 1982 until 1985.

Below
Black wool sisterhood vest matched with wide-leg culottes and black crepe button shirt. Cinched with the stainless-steel sisterhood leather belt.

of 'investing in Africa', but essentially, setting up business that mines and scavenges its resources and funnels the profits straight to the pockets of the investing country or firm. This type of investment further cripples us. It needs to be an investment that sees the human potential and allows all involved to thrive.

What is African luxury?

I feel like African craft intersects with European notions of luxury, even though people often miss the associations, because it's this idea of rarified skill, of taking time, of respecting the process. What makes them different is how the manner in which European luxury is harnessed and promoted.

How can Africa establish a foothold in the global luxury-goods economy?

By recognizing that it needs to set up its own system that can sustainably, and in as closed-loop as possible, support itself. We are not in the global North [that has had years of intentional growth in their respective fashion industries]. It is imperative that we recognize that we are at the beginning of our own renaissance and in turn, are lucky enough to set its bounds and its pace. We need to nurture it into the industry the global luxury goods economy wants to become – sustainable, cruelty-free, inclusive and diverse. We have the potential to achieve this, and I feel like this is a unique selling proposition that can propel our fledgling industry and enable us to gain a foothold in the global market.

Kat van Duinen

Founded in 2010, Kat van Duinen is a leading luxury fashion and leather-design house specializing in exceptional fabrics and exotic leather, elevated to iconography through impeccable details and precise tailoring. The brand's signature, ethically sourced exotic-leather pieces and ready-to-wear collections are underpinned by a minimalist aesthetic, and accented by a uniquely African textures such as ostrich leather, creating a delicate balance between sophistication and something quintessentially African for the global market. The brand, with its roots in Cape Town, is committed to nurturing local craftsmanship and industry, with a transparent supply chain that encompasses the sourcing of genuine exotic skins that are licensed as sustainable and GOTS (Global Organic Textile Standard) certified organic textiles. Kat van Duinen collections are an ode to strength through simplicity and timeless elegance and the brand remains true

Opposite
The Strelitzia taffeta dress in maroon and the Mini Mpumelelo bag from the New Now collection by Kat van Duinen. Mpumelelo bag in mustard-yellow python skin.

to the inherent tenets of luxury: exclusivity, quality, sustainability and exquisite craftsmanship. We are introduced to Africa's fledgling exotic-leather industry through the eyes of designer and creative director Kat van Duinen herself.

As a manufacturer of exotic-leather bags, does your supply chain look any different from that of purely fashion brands?

We manufacture both clothing and exotic-leather goods, both of which encompass different processes and supply-chain practices. We work with an incredible team of artisans specializing in exotic leather. Each exotic skin is unique and presents a peculiar challenge in the

Opposite
The Isibambo top handle bag from the Healing Energy Collection by Kat van Duinen. Composed of mustard-yellow python skin.

Right
The Ebusuku travel bag from the Blomboy X Kat van Duinen collaboration. Ebusuku bag in anthracite ostrich leather.

manufacturing process, demanding immense handcrafting skills because of the fragility of the material. The processes are undertaken predominantly by hand, with little room for automation and speed, unlike in pure fashion.

What is luxury and how is it manifested in Africa?

Luxury is increasingly shifting away from the attributes of perfection and distinction through brand positioning and pricing strategy. In the era of mechanization and mass manufacturing, the dynamics have gravitated towards products that are niche and truly handmade. With Africa possessing abundant skills in beading, weaving and metalsmithing, one can conclude that the handmade is where luxury is manifested the most in Africa. The term 'craftsmanship', however, cannot be expanded to encapsulate just about anything produced by hand, but remains the work of skilled artisans whose output can withstand the test of global quality standards. This is where the paradox lies in the context of African luxury, where the abundance of handcrafting – perhaps due to the fact that we are yet to fully industrialize – has not translated into a viable luxury industry.

How can Africa establish a foothold in the global luxury-goods market?

I believe it will take deliberate efforts to attune the abundance of handcrafting skills to luxury production if we desire a share of the global luxury market. This is achievable by upskilling, establishing standards and, in some instances, governing institutions to oversee quality standards in both the product and the local value chain. For example, we are one of a niche group of global brands that can ship genuine exotic leather worldwide. This is because the global exotic-leather industry is highly regulated, requiring certification from oversight agencies such as the Wildlife Conservation Society and local customs each time a finished product is shipped to clients. This process, however daunting, is a global 'best practice' that cannot be sidestepped if we desire to compete in the global market.

I also think a mindset shift is critical to establishing a foothold in the global luxury supply chain.

While we do have artisans with impressive skills, I find them largely disengaged from the value of their craft. This is not necessarily a matter of education, but one of mindset. Elsewhere in Europe, craftsmen take exceptional pride in their skills and attend fastidiously to every facet of the manufacturing process to ensure that each product is a masterpiece. I do not know how such pride can be instilled in traditional or indigenous craftspeople – I guess it will require broad engagement among stakeholders.

What is the impact of the influx of international brands on Africa's luxury industry?

It is a positive sign, first because it validates the local market in the face of the prevalent misconception that Africa is poor. Africa is wealthy, despite the challenges of achieving better living standards. Furthermore, the metrics for valuing wealth on the continent are often misaligned to the African context and fail to establish the truth that the high-net-worth individual in Africa is just as wealthy as the Russian oligarch or the wealthy Japanese. I think that there is a sizeable market for luxury and that consumers are discerning in taste due to the influence of electronic media and travel. Conversely, the influx of European brands also underscores the appeal of international brands for African consumers. Unlike European consumers who have mature tastes that transcend the logo, African consumers still appropriate European brands as status symbols at the expense of equally excellent African brands. It will take time to shift local tastes towards the understated and subtle nuances of indigenous brands. Overall, I think that as Europe's luxury economy stagnates, Africa is yet to experience its own luxury boom – and that is quite exciting.

Will you consider collaboration among African brands as a viable pathway to accessing global markets?

Collaboration is the buzzword of the industry and yet a far cry from reality. We are still stuck in a competitive mindset and the delusion that there is not enough market for us to co-exist or collaborate. I have suggested, for example, that exotic manufacturers in South Africa form a coalition to represent African luxury, with an imposing stand at great luxury trade shows, such as the Tranoï in Paris, or in New York, but this hasn't crystallized mainly because of the overarching desire to protect our respective clients and brand identity. However, I think that, despite serving a niche segment, each brand caters to a unique demography and exploring the synergy within our unique worldviews makes us a formidable force within the global industry, more so than in our individual capacities. Collaboration also affords us the voice to interface with policy makers and stakeholders in the supply chain to our benefit.

Layered evening gown in Tulle from the Practical
Magic Collection by Kat van Duinen. This design
comes in various colours.

Overall, we stand to gain immensely,
approaching the global market collaboratively,
rather than being disunited.

Peuhl Vagabond

Scattered across the Sahel savannah in West and Central Africa, the Peulh people (also known as the Fulani), herders, itinerant craftspeople and wealthy merchants, have contributed immensely to the material culture of Africa. Peulh Vagabond, established by Dyenaa Diaw in 2014, celebrates the rich cultural heritage of the Peulh, captured through a collection of captivating iridescent hues and striking silhouettes. Diaw trained as a fashion designer at the Paul Poiret school in Paris but pursued a career in pharmaceuticals before reverting to her original passion for design. Peulh Vagabond is as much a mission as it is a brand, one that has seen Diaw become a creative nomad, exploring indigenous African textiles, even from outside the Peulh culture to preserve and promote them. She exhibits mastery over diverse textiles, creating intriguing ensembles with woven and dyed textiles such as kente, bogolanfini, faso dan fani and koko dunda, which featured in Glaive, the SS21 collection. The brand engages in social enterprise, employing clusters of weavers and cooperatives made up mostly of women. Its signature garment, the loincloth, is made of cotton that is spun and handwoven by women in Burkina Faso. Here, Diaw speaks about the aspects of culture and storytelling that go into building a global luxury brand.

What is the role of African culture in building a successful fashion brand?

Culture is at the centre of the Peulh Vagabond collections. I essentially draw on my roots to create captivating stories, cognizant of the fact that African culture is sidelined in the global

Opposite
'Tawi' mesh 3D robe from the SS21 Glaive collection by Peulh Vagabond. This collection is a tribute to the work of dyers. It highlights the knotting techniques that creates the beautiful patterns of 'Koko Dunda' a dyed textile from Burkina Faso. Kôkô Dunda means 'The entrance to Kôkô', named after the district of Bobo where the dyers who specialize in its manufacture traditionally work.

economy. I think that, because of this, Peulh Vagabond tries, through art, fashion and many other means, to reappropriate its own history. Through Peulh Vagabond, I am able to revive the ancient histories of our ancestors and endangered indigenous textiles and crafts with an eye that is ultra-contemporary.

I often quote President Mobutu who, in a speech at the United Nations in 1973, defined 'culture and authenticity' as the source of conscience, a means for people to seek the value of their ancestors in order to appreciate those who had contributed to their country's harmonious and natural development. He steadfastly believed in the importance of preserving indigenous culture and resisting blindly importing foreign ideologies into Zaire (now the Democratic Republic of the Congo). And, without culture as an anchor, no brand can succeed in the highly competitive global fashion economy.

What role does storytelling play in projecting African excellence in your product?

Each collection is an opportunity for me to travel and meet people with a new craft or architecture. To create, I need to be in contact with the actors of my inspirations. I observe them, I glean knowledge from them and I also learn from my own history, as well as that of humanity. It's not just about making clothes for the sake of making clothes. Storytelling, on the other hand, is about animating and bringing into the spotlight the hidden treasures of Africa,

Casual blazer and pants in Koko Dunda by Kat van Duinen.

which are worth their weight in gold. Far from the fast-fashion sphere, these people have managed to keep the authenticity of beautiful things and, in terms of ecological impact, will pass on a legacy of preserving the world: Burkina Faso and its woven cotton fabrics that are kept for life; Mali and its hand-hammered jewellery; Mauritania and its dyed cotton veils, and so on. But the most important thing is that they have been able to create and organize themselves into cooperatives, and that all these hands manage to support entire families.

What is African luxury?

Luxury in Africa simply means the future, and the fashion sector can contribute positively to the development of the African continent. The biggest fashion houses have understood this. They see it as a godsend and are starting to establish themselves on the continent, following the example of Saint Laurent Paris or Louis Vuitton, and many others. Africa is also very attractive for retail, which is a godsend for designers who are starting out with a smaller budget or without investors on their side.

Long shunned by investors, the African continent is now appealing to global brands. With half of the population now under twenty years old and fifty cities with more than a million inhabitants, Africa offers a huge pool of consumers. Moreover, the Black woman has always been, in my eyes, a lover of things of value; she has a sharp eye and is very fashionable. I believe Black women are inventive tastemakers, who do not necessarily pander to the validation of Western media. As a young Senegalese evolving in Paris, I possess this savoir faire which I apply in defining a contemporary

vision of a chic cosmopolitan African lady. I revisit the wardrobe of my parents often for inspiration, drawing from the glamorous styles of a bygone era. I am inspired not only by my mother, but all her contemporaries who influenced my youth, both in Senegal and other parts of the continent. Africa is my DNA.

I note, however, that both schools of styling and quality models must be created in order to encourage authentic African ready-to-wear brands, to strengthen the competitiveness

of the local textile industry and adapt it to the international market and, to achieve this essential progress, the participation of governments is necessary.

How can Africa position its local industries at the forefront of the evolving global luxury industry?

An industry usually starts locally and then builds globally over time. This is what Africa is clearly lacking. These things should be decided

Opposite
The Sundiata sweater in black by Kat van Duinen. The sweater is detailed with hand painted motif drawn from the artistic heritage of the Mandingo Empire.

Above
The robe Tougan from the Midnight hour capsule collection by Kat van Duinen. Black-and-green striped midi dress with V neck, and a ball effect skirt. The robe Tougan is composed of hand-woven faso dan fani produced by craft women in Burkina Faso.

at state level, as is the case in Ghana or Nigeria. Francophone Africa is still too timid. Many African countries are still captive to the global economy. For this to change, it is important that we pursue strategies for industrial and economic growth that are best suited to the continent's peculiar situation. Furthermore, local industries will remain underdeveloped if African countries fail to curtail the export of valuable raw materials cheaply to the global market.

Tokyo James

Shuttling between Lagos and London, designer Iniye Tokyo James explores the commonality that exists across different cultures, genders and lifestyles. James credits his British and Nigerian heritage for his bold and evocative design sensibilities, mixing punk with the structured look of British tailoring. James uses an expansive range of indigenous African textiles, such as the Aso Oke, to dramatic effect, while experimenting extensively with leather. His irreverence for orthodoxy is evident in the edgy and gender-fluid pieces that have become his trademark. In each collection, James explores the intersectionality of seeming opposites – old and new, simplicity and complexity, good and bad – and Africa and Europe. Since its inception in 2015, Tokyo James has received much acclaim, featuring in *Vogue, i-D, Harpers Bazaar UK, W magazine, Highsnobiety* and many other publications. James has, since 2019, embarked on a bold

initiative to source labour and materials in Africa – an initiative that has required substantial capital investment and the upskilling of local craftspeople.

As a brand that operates in two distinctive localities, how have you managed sourcing in Africa?
It is about training, and we have injected significant amounts of capital and resources to upskill our artisans to the standard we require. It is not easy – more so with the challenges associated with the rhythm of local artisans. But the result has been quite astonishing. For example, many of our consumers believe that the Ata Rodo bag, which has become an icon of the brand, are made in Europe, but it is actually

Opposite
A lace jacket with gold band detailing from the SS22 collection by Tokyo James. It is accessorized with the iconic Ata Rodo bag.

Above
'No one cares' suit from the SS17 collection by Tokyo James. Tokyo James experiments with effervescent hues and thought-provoking quotes delivered with a twist of humour. The brand delivers on its promise of impeccable structure, detail and fit.

Above, right
Suede trench coat from the SS17 collection by Tokyo James.

Opposite
Loose weave jersey suit from the SS21 collection by Tokyo James. This pieces shows off Tokyo James's dexterity with unconventional materials, delivering structure and form to the fragile see-through woven jersey fabric.

happening in our studios in Lagos. They are shocked at the quality that we have been able to achieve in this part of the world, and yet all of it is down to my artisans. The process is pretty much experimental: we exchange ideas until we find the best approach, one that suits everybody and, ultimately, the consumer.

What is luxury and how has it manifested in Africa?

Luxury for me is attention to detail, quality in fabrics, simplicity in design – however, you need a balance between simplicity and creating a 'wow' factor. It is easy to do loud, but quite difficult to achieve the opposite. There has always been African luxury; it has existed, but has not been celebrated. It is evident across the continent and globally, both in how we have inspired global brands and in our mastery of crafts such as beading, weaving and goldsmithing, among many others. More importantly, luxury in Africa is characterized by the norms of sustainability and the cultural values that have accompanied them. Since antiquity, we have interacted with materials and nature differently; they were sacred to us and this urge for unbridled consumption in contemporary times is foreign to us. Through our approach to materials amid the abundance of valuable natural resources, I am convinced that luxury has its origins in Africa.

Is Africa positioned to compete in the global luxury economy?

Yes, we are, but we also have to educate our populace. The definition of luxury has largely been shaped by Western media, and this remains a missing link in Africa. We are bombarded with images of Western luxury, but that needs to change and we need our populace to be informed. The exploits of European brands are adequately archived and taught to the next generation of designers. Prominent European brands are celebrated and sustained through a global language of luxury. It is also about patronizing what emanates from Africa: African consumers need to be educated that what we have is equally valuable. Indeed, as African designers, we have to invest ten times more than their counterparts in other parts of the world to achieve the same level of quality and brand allure.

How should Africa assert its place in the world of global luxury?

We have to start creating more spaces and interacting with ourselves more often as designers. Furthermore, our local brands are not as widely distributed across the continent. It is imperative to have access to more retail spaces to enable the African consumer to engage with brands from every part of the continent and this comes down to investment.

Black patent-leather trapunto pattern pants and plain vest, ensemble accessorized with the iconic Ata Rodo Bag by Tokyo James.

Maison ARTC

Artsi Ifrach is no conventional designer. His brand, Maison ARTC, headquartered in Marrakech, Morocco, is a lesson in history, culture, travel and sustainability. The vibrant colours, eclectic styles and nostalgic themes emerge unscripted from the hands of a creative genius with the most striking results. At Maison ARTC, no two items are the same as each piece – formed out of vintage cloth sourced on Ifrach's numerous travels – undergoes the techniques of layering, appliqué, patchwork and beading. Maison ARTC uses fashion to preserve both the literal cloth pieces of cast-off garments and the history of the cultures they embody. Ifrach's works are as irreverent as they are philosophical; he is a self-confessed autodidact who eschews the motions of fashion, rather employing his craft to interrogate identity, spirituality and sensitive social issues, such as the mindlessness of capitalism. His greatest fascination is with the

burqa, an intriguing piece of clothing found in almost every country in Africa. To him, the burqa, which has become an iconography of Maison ARTC, is at once mysterious and ambiguous.

What inspired the establishment of your brand?

There are three codewords for my practice: art, culture and education. As a person who is well attuned to culture, I make custom pieces – one-of-a-kind garments for my clients out of respect for their personality and irrespective of their status. I perceive every client as belonging to their own self-constructed universe and having

Opposite
Woven Moroccan textile gown with puffed and ruffled satin sleeves, accessorized with embroidered pontifical cap and crown by Maison ARTC. Here, Artsi Ifrach tinkers with the idea of politics and religion.

their own idea of how they want to portray themselves. My approach to design is deliberately slow and intrinsically sustainable – my sustainable ethos is propelled by the urge to add value to the intangible aspects of our life that are easily forgotten. Through my work, I want to remind people of the past, asserting a revival of the old, juxtaposed with the new.

Do you think a sustainable fashion future is possible?

I will sound somewhat critical: the world is abuzz with theories about sustainability, but not many are sincerely committed to the cause. The biggest enemy of fashion is fashion, and sustainability itself has become a marketing gimmick to sell more and more clothes, and that is where I diverge from mainstream fashion. Being sustainable demands a slow and mindful approach to making. To be sustainable you have, literally, to stop producing and interrogate what motivates you to create more clothes. Because these demands are difficult, I fear a truly sustainable fashion future is impossible. What will make the difference, in my opinion, is for the behemoth brands to scale back, for globalization to slow down, for smaller designers to take responsibility for making and creating mindfully. I can

Opposite
Burqa composed of re-purposed textile by Maison ARTC. The Burqa features predominantly as the iconography of Maison ARTC, an omnipresent piece of religious clothing across the continent of Africa. Artsi Ifrach is fascinated by the burqa for its enigmatic quality.

Above, right
Yellow cab dress by Maison ARTC. This design is reminiscent of New York's ubiquitous yellow taxis.

confidently claim that my brand is 100 percent sustainable, but there aren't many brands like mine out there, and I cannot make all the difference alone.

You are proposing that brands slow down, but in a world where growth targets are fundamental, do you consider slow fashion to be a viable business model?

Fashion is a commercial industry, one that transcends the demand–supply dynamics to manifest the most bizarre form of manipulation. In the fashion industry, planned obsolescence is

accepted as the norm – we have in the past decade moved from two major fashion seasons to almost five, all in a quest to sell more and more clothes. So, any designer that moves to the rhythm of the global fashion economy will struggle to adopt a model that sounds counterintuitive. So, yes, slow fashion is a viable model, however it is only suitable for designers that are attuned to the needs of the environment. I always insist I am not in the fashion industry: I am into fashion. For example, my fidelity to a sustainable ethos limits my capacity to grow beyond a certain threshold, and that is acceptable because it is innate in my identity and ethos as a brand. I desire, rather, to make things that are inspirational and to offer a sublime, almost spiritual, experience to people. And it is fulfilling, to grow consistently and at a determined pace, but this is just not the case with everybody – the designer needs to understand their own pathway to growth and must appreciate the cost of that decision.

What is African luxury?

First, I believe luxury is subjective, however, as Africans we are submerged in such remarkable culture and that, for me, is luxury in itself. The same liberty to experience culture is absent in many other parts of the world, where the remnants of indigenous cultures are confined behind glass façades in museums. On the contrary, we *are* the culture and can buy and enjoy whatever we want, so long as it is good for us. But it behoves us, as a people and especially as designers, to interrogate and project authentic African culture if we desire to build luxury that is uniquely African.

What can Africa do to contribute to the global luxury economy?

I do not think it is appropriate to ask what Africa can do for the global luxury economy, because we have done so much for it already. I only hope that Africa will learn to claim its contribution for itself and not give it up, like it means nothing.

What is the most iconic piece of Maison ARTC?

I create the burqa because I want to change the idea behind it, as many people have misconceptions that it is exclusively Islamic and oppressive to women. But I say no, it is seen all over Africa, it is beautiful, it is mysterious, it is poetic and I play around with it a lot. I think it is timeless, a canvas of imagination and the abstract, and I am particularly intrigued by the dialogue that it engenders: 'I see you, but you can only imagine who I am'.

In 'solitude' by Masion ARTC. Model draped in large motif crocheted cape, white cotton shirt with fringed cuffs and accessorized with lace headwrap.

Imane Ayissi

A red-carpet favourite of Zendaya and Angela Bassett, Imane Ayissi is a trailblazing designer delivering a complex and contemporary vision of couture. Having worked initially as a model for designers such as Alphadi, Seidu Keïta and Kofi Ansah, Imane Ayissi has witnessed the changing phases of African fashion, he is just as much a pioneering figure of its history. Practising now as a designer in his Parisian atelier, the Cameroon-born designer creates masterpieces that encapsulate Africa's inimitable spirit and captivating craft cultures. Established in 2004, the Imane Ayissi brand is a modern experimental take on ancient indigenous African textiles, pared down to appeal to a global clientele. The brand's signature pieces include ready-to-wear cocktail dresses made from faso dan fani, an indigenous textile of the Marka people of Burkina Faso. The Ghanaian kente, Malian bogolonfini and the Cameroonian ndop are a few of Ayissi's favourite textiles.

In 2020, Imane Ayissi's perseverance paid off when he was eventually invited to showcase his work as a guest designer on the official schedule of the Fédération de la Haute Couture et de la Mode (FHCM). Given the exacting standards and stringent regulations of the FHCM, it was a testament to the designer's hard work, ingenuity and excellence as a couturier of global repute. As only the third African couturier (after Alphadi and Noureddine Amir) to have graced the couture runway in the over one-and-a-half-century existence of the FHCM, Ayissi is cognizant of his crucial responsibility as an ambassador for Africa, and

Opposite
Tiered peplum dress composed of cotton and dyed raffia yarns from the Madzang collection AW21-22 by Imane Ayissi. 'Madzang' in the Ewondo language of central Cameroon refers to a family member with whom there is complicity. The collection explores our relationship to people of distinct tribes, cultures, religions and race, with whom we share common experiences.

seeks to project a continent reimagined on the merits of its craftsmanship, creativity and know-how.

What is the guiding philosophy of Imane Ayissi and what impact does this have on your product and the supply chain?

First, I think fashion must transcend the simple creation of nice clothes to pursue some form of social activism. Through my work, I have chosen to highlight African cultures, talent and craftsmanship to actively reshape the global narrative on Africa. Secondly, my work evokes femininity – although I also design a bit of menswear, I always attribute my main inspiration to my mother, so my brand is about female empowerment, independent and free women, including the idea of freedom of women's bodies. Thirdly, is the concept of a responsible industry. I don't think the fashion industry should continue to pollute our planet, so it is important for me to minimize the impact of my designs on the environment. All my collections include materials and textiles produced in African countries, and, since almost all the indigenous textile industry has disappeared in African countries, I work mostly with artisans, who I have to find and, sometimes, train.

Tunic made from custom-woven kente fabric for Madzang Collection AW21-22, by Imane Ayissi.

Your brand sources in Africa and sells to global markets. How do you balance the demands of these two worlds?

Technically, it makes the way I work and manage my brand more difficult than non-African luxury brands, because I work with artisans who are sometimes in small cities or villages in different African countries, with textiles that are usually not made for

contemporary, industrially produced apparel. For example, the kente and faso dan fani I use often in my collections are woven in small widths, while all contemporary apparel is constructed from fabrics 1.4 metres wide, so I have to think of that when I design the patterns for my garments. I also have to train the artisans so that they can reach the international standard for luxury in terms of quality, attention to detail, consistency and finishing. Even the idea of reproducing exactly the same fabric several times is not something obvious for the artisans I work with.

I also have to balance things in term of style, and that is sometimes difficult: of course, I want to show true African cultures, but I have also to distil it in a manner that makes my designs understandable and desirable to the rest of the world. Finding this equilibrium can be quite difficult … where I am able to project and celebrate African traditions in a contemporary way without undermining its true beauty and complexity. But it means also working against the clichés attached to African cultures (about colours or colour harmony, for example) that even Africans themselves have embraced.

Your invitation to the FHCM is a testament to your hard work and excellence as a designer. What impact does this achievement have on Africa's cultural renaissance?

I hope it can help to change representation of African cultures and societies. My biggest challenge is the misconception that the idea of luxury is not compatible with African culture, except when raw materials, such as gold and diamonds, are involved. This is because African craftmanship, know-how and talent are underestimated not only globally but also by African governments and authorities. Of course, things are changing and a lot of contemporary artists from many African countries are well recognized, but the contemporary art world celebrates only a handful of phenomenal Black artists; fashion, on the other hand, has the

advantage of being somewhat broad and diverse. That's why it was so important for me to be part of the haute couture calendar since it is seen as the highest level of fashion, with an idea of perfect craftmanship. So, I am, for example, quite proud of an article about my works in a Japanese newspaper or of my dresses worn by Chinese celebrities, because I hope it can help to change the image of African cultures, not only in Europe but also globally.

You explored the commonalities of cultures the world over in Madzang, the AW21/22 collection. Did you conceive it as a means of fostering empathy and a greater sense of humanity amid the global pandemic?

Maybe I was inspired by the impact of the pandemic, with the same consequences all over the world that show we are one humanity. But, maybe, it is also that I am a bit afraid that the completely legitimate fight for equality could end in a violent competition between different minority communities. Fighting for the recognition of value in African cultures doesn't mean I want to start a war against Western societies, or that I want to trivialize other cultures. When I see how polarized American society is, I am afraid that it could become a dominant model for African societies and, especially, African youth. However, I believe that what we have in common is just as important as our differences, and we can see different cultures as the diversity inherent to the human race. Since the culture of appearance is common to every human culture, it is easy to highlight the commonalities of different cultures with fashion.

What is African luxury and in what peculiar ways is it manifested?

As it is everywhere, it is rarity, exquisite craftmanship, specific know-how, tradition and innovation at the same time, and, above all, the idea that objects (garments, accessories) carry meanings, sense, histories. With the globalization and industrialization of luxury goods, I have the feeling that most of the international luxury brands are losing their meaning. What is still particular in our African societies is that all the precious objects we produce are still full of symbols, meanings and histories. Even if they are not completely understandable to everyone, it gives them a very specific value.

Is Africa adequately positioned to compete as a source of luxury goods for the global market?

I would say Africa could potentially become a source of luxury goods, but it won't become a reality without education and investment. The French luxury industry is so strong because, from King Louis XIV (d. 1715) to contemporary rivals Bernard Arnault (chief executive of LVMH) and François Pinault (chair of luxury group Kering), both institutions and businesspeople have been aware of the economic impact and soft power of the luxury industry. Unfortunately, it is still not the case in African countries, where governments and businesspeople still don't consider the luxury industry as a serious economic sector.

How can Africa contribute to recalibrating the global luxury economy in the coming decades?

The world is spiralling out of control at dizzying speed due to the vagaries of capitalism and overconsumption, thanks to the presently entrenched culture of instant gratification, we are depleting our natural resources faster than we can replenish them. Unless we slow down and recalibrate, we could encounter yet another global catastrophe. I think it is imperative that we consider the impact of our lifestyle on the environment, in order to consume less and better. It is also incumbent on designers to create with intent, emphasizing quality and longevity of garments above the ephemerality of fashion. This is where Africa, with its

Couture by Imane Ayissi. These designs are showcased at the FHCM show in Paris to critical acclaim. Imani Ayissi adapts cultural forms and materials peculiar to Africa into striking and modern pieces –the hallmark of experience, creativity and excellence.

relatively less-industrialized manufacturing economies can shine: by adopting consumption practices that are antithetic to the status quo and building a truly sustainable industry that the rest of the world can learn from.

Taibo Bacar

Founded in 2008 by Taibo Bacar and Tatiana Ismael, Taibo Bacar is a luxury brand based in Maputo, the capital city of Mozambique. The brand caters to the sophisticated woman, delicately blending couture and classic ready-to-wear. Designer and creative director, Taibo Bacar, grew up with the sound of his mother's sewing machine. Despite a brief stint in IT, he ventured into fashion, studying at the prestigious Istituto Marangoni in Milan. Named as the Emerging Designer of the Year 2012 at the African Fashion International Fashion Week in South Africa, Taibo Bacar has shown at almost every prestigious fashion event including Lagos, New York, London, Paris and Milan Fashion Weeks. Taibo Bacar employs a wide range of textures, indigenous textiles and techniques to produce a clean and flattering silhouette. The brand draws from the rich cultural heritage of Mozambique, a country that served as a major entrepôt for traders from

Central Africa, Egypt, Arabia, India and the Persian Gulf. The brand also offers a range of ready-to-wear accessories such as sunglasses, clutches and belts.

Taibo Bacar is known for its clean silhouette, exquisite detailing, captivating textures, and understated elegance, what philosophy underpins your design practice?
Taibo Bacar has, for years, focused and extolled three key elements when it comes to its philosophy and brand identity, those being: quality of high-end pieces, Mozambican heritage and customs, and the female silhouette. Elegance has turned into a reference

Opposite
Black dress shirt from the Safari collection by Taibo Bacar.

point in the brand's DNA, and we aim to showcase exactly that in Taibo Bacar's design practice, regardless of which piece is being made.

What do you consider as the most fundamental pillars in positioning a brand as 'luxury'?

At Taibo Bacar luxury is directly connected to beauty, and that's what we aim to deliver. We also have a mission in writing a new history in

Above (left to right)
Balalaica denim jacket and pant from the Transition collection by Taibo Bacar.

Opposite
Men's camel blazer accessorized with eyewear and ladies tweed jacket by Taibo Bacar.

the luxury books, a mission to reshape the perspective of fashion in Africa (to the world) and it's fair to say that having that goal has helped us establish and position the brand on the luxurious side of fashion.

What is African luxury and in what ways is it manifested?

No matter where, luxury is luxury. The difference is in who practices and who manifests it. African luxury is solely a term used to define workings of luxury practised by Africans or with African heritage and customs and a huge part of what is considered African luxury is exactly that: movements directly linked to African culture and its people.

There is a need for us to evolve as part of globalization and since culture is static but art and luxury dynamic, we must consider that African luxury is synonymous with the behaviour of all African luxury lovers and users.

What does it take to build a luxury brand in Africa?

Building and establishing a luxury brand is in itself a challenge. In Africa this challenge becomes even more demanding because of the devaluation of African brands, the constant comparison with renowned international brands, and political issues among other factors. Essentially, we believe it takes guts to face a market so demanding. After that, it's a lot of learning to know the end consumer, and accepting and filtering of opinions, whether these come from professionals or the clientele. It's also important to discover and be certain of what the DNA of the brand is, that way it's easier to set goals and objectives and to focus on working to achieve them and ultimately building your luxury brand.

Opposite
Custom-print wrap dress by Taibo Bacar.

Above
Transition chiffon shirt and skirt with Yani bag in python brown by Taibo Bacar.

How can Africa establish a foothold in the global luxury economy?
The important bit in this process is having a larger number of makers in the industry; it's having creatives understand that they too can take their brand to high-end points and that it's possible to create luxury within our culture without completely westernizing it or losing identity. Africa's greatest asset is its tradition, and we need to start appreciating it more. That's the only way other people will start appreciating it too.

Johanna Bramble

Through the hands of textile designer Johanna Bramble and her Dakar-based eponymous brand, African textiles are undergoing a revival at the intersection of tradition and modernity. Drawn to the evocative patterns, indigenous knowledge systems and techniques of weaving in Africa, she skipped a lucrative career in Parisian haute couture to establish her studio in Dakar. Although the studio launched officially in 2013, Bramble has since 2009 worked closely with indigenous Senegalese weavers, upskilling them in modern techniques and product development. From its studios in Dakar, the brand has collaborated with numerous other brands to produce textiles for furnishing and interiors, as well as fashion.

Bramble is passionate about social impact and the sustenance of indigenous textile heritage. Her work also advances the frontiers of traditional techniques and knowledge systems through experimentations with both

synthetic and natural fibres, for example pioneering the research and development of indigenous fibres. Bramble also works with Manjak weavers, a group of master weavers from the Casamance region of southern Senegal and Guinea-Bissau.

What inspired your journey into textile design?

Textile craft is something I inherited from my mother, who practised weaving as a hobby. She was also deeply into the arts and interior design; she was tasteful in her choice of colours and textures and that rubbed off on me. I set out initially to pursue a career as an interior architect; however, I noticed I was drawn more to textile craft as it came a lot more naturally, perhaps because of my prior exposure to it. I also felt that textiles, especially when used as clothing, served a need that was far more personal and emotional to people and I saw

within this an opportunity to leverage my creativity to fulfil an important need of humanity. Textile for me is a language on its own. Indeed, all the civilizations around the world have their own language around textile and that is what makes my career rewarding, since I can partake through each piece I make in the many aspirations and emotions of the people that wear them everywhere in the world.

Is there any particular material that you consider as central to your work?

Considering the phenomenon of climate change, I am particularly concerned about the impact of my craft on the environment, which causes me to consider natural fibres –

especially organic and hand-spun indigenous cotton that are ancient to Senegal. Other fibres that are particuliar to our region [and] which I am currently experimenting with are baobab fibre, sabra fibre, which is extracted from the aloe vera plant, [as well as] banana fibre and typha fibre. I am also drawn to indigenous textiles because of my mission to empower local craftspeople, comprising guilds of women weavers. However, my skill as a designer enables me to innovate and create using unconventional materials, materials that, in my opinion, are more sustainable. For example, in a recent project for a custom interior design work, I used the coils of discarded vintage cassette tapes to weave a truly distinctive

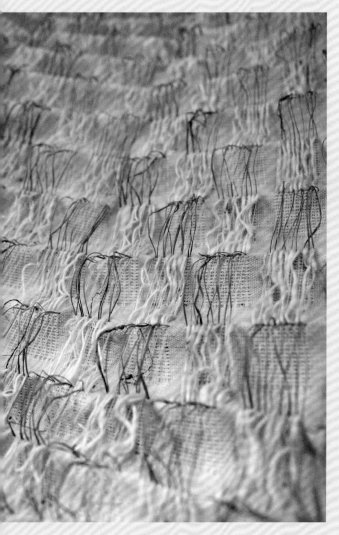

Pages 169, 170, 171
Experimental and artistic development of woven
textiles for the 2022 home and fashion textile collection
by Johanna Bramble.

Above, left
Elastane and abaca fibre (from banana) interspersed atop
indigenous hand-woven cotton by Johanna Bramble.

Above, right
Elastane and raffia fibre interspersed atop indigenous
hand-woven cotton by Joahnna Bramble.

textile. Of the many works that I do, I find such
unconventional projects the most engaging.

What do you consider as unique to Africa's textile heritage?

What I find unique to Africa is the energy that is
infused into the textile craft. By energy, I mean
the cultural and symbolic values as well as the
performative approach to weaving that
animates the craft and imparts to each piece a
semblance of a soul. For example, among
cultures such as the Dogon of Mali, the Igbo of
Nigeria and the Kano, textiles were not merely
items of commerce, but also featured
prominently in rituals and ancestral ceremonies

and their production occurred performatively to soulful rhythm and folklore. It is not surprising that African art wrought through forms like weaving have inspired many of the world's distinguished artists and designers, including the venerable Picasso. The types of indigenous materials also distinguish African textiles, with each region possessing the expertise in one medium or another. The materials themselves belong to the broader cosmology of the weaving craft. Being cognizant of this unique energy greatly influences how I approach my work, where instead of masking the imperfections of this energy, I allow them a safe passage. The result is a truly magnificent, textiles that are imprinted with the cultural heritage and the personal stories of individual weavers.

Do recent advancements in textile technology constitute an opportunity or a threat to indigenous textile crafts and cultures?

I think it is essential that we rethink the relationship between craft and technology; they need not be antagonistic, and when approached the right way can be complementary. This is most important in the processing of indigenous materials where modern research could play an important role. I have observed from my recent experimentations that most indigenous natural fibres require further refinement, necessitating some form of modernized technologies. This is where I believe localized solutions and technology can intersect. I have also observed a synergy between indigenous knowledge systems, materials and emergent technologies, and it is important that they are harnessed in a manner that is considerate to the cultures and ecosystems of Africa.

What do you consider the most pressing challenges to Africa's indigenous textile cultures?

In Senegal, weaving is a craft dominated by men and it is transferred from father to son. However, in recent times the pride associated with weaving is diminishing and that I think is a major challenge to the sustenance of indigenous weaving cultures, because the transmission of the skill from father to son is becoming rare. This may also be linked to the unattractive remuneration associated with the trade, which is forcing many people to consider alternative careers to weaving.

Can Africa establish a competitive advantage in the global luxury economy by harnessing the potential of our textile heritage?

Of course, we can! Because no other continent wields as much diverse knowledge and know-how, and so many possibilities regarding the different weaving techniques as Africa. However, establishing a competitive advantage with our indigenous textiles will require deliberate strategies and concerted efforts in research and development. Our indigenous textile industries cannot remain in obscurity, or independent of advancing technologies, if we desire to become relevant in the global luxury industry.

T-Michael

Beyond his quirky style and iconic look, designer, tailor and filmmaker T-Michael embodies a profound creative philosophy that has underpinned his meteoric rise in the world of luxury menswear. T-Michael, who prides in his craft as a tailor, opened his first studio in 1996 and co-founded Norwegian Rain with Alexander Helle almost a decade and half later. In the orthodox realm of luxury menswear where sharply tailored Savile Row suits hold sway, only someone with such unparalleled

Right
Kalaf Angelo, musician, writer, poet, in the Davies Tuxedo, cut in black barathea from the AW 2014 collection by T-Michael.

Opposite
The versatile T Tote bag in pebbled calf leather by T-Michael.

technical proficiency and creative acumen as T-Michael could disrupt the status quo while upholding its impeccable standards. Renowned for his Scandinavian approach to design, his influences are broader, benefiting from a multiplicity of cultures, from the style etiquette of a Londoner to the creative flair of his African heritage. His creative experimentations have resulted in a collection of beautiful and functional products, such as suits, shirts, bags, hats, sunglasses and shoes, which are sold online and in the flagship stores of T-Michael / Norwegian Rain in Bergen, Oslo, Tokyo and Paris.

T-Michael's considered and unconventional approach to tailoring has warmed many hearts, including Takayuki Yajima of Y. & Sons, Yamato dynasty, a traditional kimono maker headquartered in Kanda. The result of the kindred creative ethos between T-Michael and Yajima San was the historic reinterpretation of the traditional Japanese kimono into a wardrobe staple for the contemporary man. The original T-Kimono is made from a custom-made single-striped wool-flannel suit material, that drapes in a bold and structured manner mimicking the western tailored suit. The T-Kimono, which was judged as the best designed product by *Time Out* magazine in 2017 has become a bridge between young Japanese and the ancient kimono tradition. In 2020 the Victoria and Albert Museum acquired the original T-Kimono for its permanent collection and showcased it alongside the works of design luminaries Paul Poiret, Rei Kawakubo and Yohji Yamamoto who are renowned for their take on the ancient kimono tradition.

You are revered for your culturally attuned creative sensibilities and experimental, yet structured approach to menswear. Who is T-Michael and what inspired your journey in fashion?
Quite simply, I am someone seeking to find the

Opposite
The 441 Tunic by T-Michael. The tunic is shown among Henrik Håkansson's 101 Tree Branches and Boughs at Tårnsalen Kode 4 Bergen.

Above
The iconic Norwegian Rain Raincho and Sonja Wanda from the AW 2013 collection by T-Michael.

truth in fashion and clothing, and all the while trying to define what that means as well. I was born in Ghana, I moved to London and later to Norway some thiry-two years ago. However, my journey as a professional fashion designer started in Norway, where I trained as a tailor and set up a studio. While a student, I approached fashion unconventionally, allowing my curiosity to transcend the knowledge of garments to encompass an understanding of how things were built. I opened up my studio in 1996 and made the first T-Michael collection, which was based on everything I liked to wear and a couple more years later started Norwegian Rain with Alexander Helle. Norwegian Rain was born out of a well-considered creative solution to a problem that is particuliar to Bergen, where it rains for two out of every three days. The brand's ever-expanding global appeal, is a testament to how a thoughtful solution to a local problem can resonate around the world. Obviously between the start and now I have also made shoes, and bags and dabbled in short films, all of which gravitate towards the singular objective of exploring a worldview through multiple visual narrative and mediums.

What fascinates me is the cultures through which you have moved – your African heritage, and your time in London, which explain your passion for the structured Savile Row tailoring and your exploits in Norway and, ultimately, your connection to Japan. How have these multiple cultures influenced your practice?
Yes, I believe moving through these different locales inspires and taints you at the same time. While in Norway, I observed how differently they dressed from London, a contrast of the sharp, edgy, structured look of Londoners against the soft, muted, functional and often pared-down aesthetic of the Scandinavians. These influences underpin my conceptual approach to menswear, something I call 'Scandinavian approach' because I want the suit or the garment to have a functional appeal, without compromising on style. I may also distinguish my pieces based on the fabric or the cut, and that is where my Ghanaian heritage filters through. For example, I have this piece called the Batwing, a draping garment that was inspired by the Ghanaian *Batakari*. I only removed a few of the seams from the sides and front, put a belt to it and that was it, but it is almost instinctively perceived as Japanese, and a play on the imagination is something I enjoy.

There are other pieces, like a version of our new oversize bomber jacket I call the King Size Okada and the Asafo Pants all of which are reminiscent of my Ghanaian heritage.

What is Norwegian Rain doing differently to foster a truly sustainable fashion future?
Sustainability has been at the heart of my work since the very beginning. My T-Michael Collection were limited runs made by smaller factories that used a limited stock of fabrics, this approach diminishes the likelihood of an overstock and mark downs. At Norwegian Rain, our mission from inception was to ensure that every garment has a minimal carbon footprint, and that meant seeking eco-friendly materials, with top-of-the-range Japanese fabrics composed of recycled or organic materials that are devoid of harmful substances. We are doing more by confronting overproduction and recently introduced a new concept called the compact store, where a limited selection of items in-store form the foundation of our retail operation. This is based on the concept of 'mottainai': the art of not being wasteful. The client can access information on each item by scanning a QR code on the label before placing their orders, which is delivered either from our central warehouse or delivered between four to six weeks if it is made to order. Shipping still remains a problem, but a marginal one in comparison to what would be the case if we overproduced.

What is your definition of luxury and how does it manifest in Africa?
Traditionally, luxury has been defined by opulence, and profligacy, but then it is guilted

The 441 Tunic in irish linen, Holland & Sherry for T-Michael SS21.

The Malcom double-breasted Jacket in chunky calvary twill from the AW20 collection by T-Michael.

and it taints ultimately. Luxury for me is the freedom to choose and indulge as you want without conforming to the status quo. A bespoke suit, for example, is luxury, you might pay a little bit more for it but fifteen years down the line you will still be wearing it as it is built to last. Some may opine that it is easy to aspire to that kind of luxury when you are well off, but that is not the case, back in Ghana, people make their clothing to order and they aren't necessarily the wealthiest, which demystifies the concept of luxury as the privilege of the elite. And this is where African luxury departs from the western conceptualization of the term. Through the peculiar modalities of consumption, we make it emphatically clear that luxury can be accessible, when it is stripped of all the guilted materials – the superficial things that overwhelm the product – to its simplest, most honest and truthful form. Luxury is also personal, like my ceramic cup, which is broken, and I have fixed it and even made it more beautiful by putting gold detailing in those cracks, it has evolved from an object or a mere product to an extension of myself. As a tailor, luxury is creating clothing that is worn for the next ten seasons; luxury is the truth we put in clothing, or any other object for that matter.

Mimi Plange

Born in Ghana and based in New York, Mimi Plange's design approach is bold and irreverent, a fusion of American sportswear classics, couture and punk. Plange nurtured her creative prowess in the Bay Area at The University of California, Berkeley, where she earned a degree in Architecture and later, a post graduate degree in Fashion Design at the Fashion Institute of Design and Merchandising (FIDM) in San Francisco. She then moved to New York and launched her eponymous brand in 2010.

Despite growing up in California and operating in New York, Mimi identifies strongly with her Ghanaian and African heritage, she draws inspiration from the culture, folklore and eclectic cityscapes of the continent. Her Autumn/Winter collection, 'Scarred Perfection,' for example, explored scarification, where she adapted trapunto on leather to mimic and elevate the beauty of a culture that once evoked pride among indigenous tribes throughout Africa. Plange's collections feature textures, clean lines and details that drape the feminine body gracefully, demonstrating her mastery of structured and deconstructed silhouettes. However, she is unimpressed by the status quo and is constantly evolving. Plange identifies as a design rebel who speaks back at fashion, questioning its precepts in the philosophy of 'unfashion' a term that she coined to describe 'the outsider' who charts her own path, undesirous of validation, and in pursuit of her own identity.

Opposite
Nuba T from the Unfashion collection by Mimi Plange. Leather trim nylon mesh T-shirt dress with neon spikes and metal rings, worn over a backless turtleneck, neon maxi dress. Unfashion is a movement, based on identity, distinction and individuality. Its story of freedom is expressed through diverse creative and design aesthetics, such as the body adornment and body painting.

Plange has collaborated with famed shoe designer Manolo Blahnik, iconic design brand Roche Bobois, Instagram, LeBron James and Nike. She participated in the Celebration of Design Event hosted by First Lady Michelle Obama atnhe White House, and her award-winning designs have been worn by Mrs Obama, Angela Bassett, Awkwafina, Regina King, Serena Williams, Rihanna, Gabriel Union-Wade, and Viola Davis.

What inspired your decision to pursue fashion after graduating with a degree in Architecture?

I've wanted to be a fashion designer since I was twelve years old. I spent a good amount of time plotting and scheming about how I was going to make my dream a reality when I was little. My mom didn't think fashion was a great career because it wasn't stable enough, but I wasn't willing to let it go. I decided I would still pursue fashion, but wanted to also have something to fall back on just in case. I used to love reading fashion magazines and came across a bio of the late Italian Designer, Gianfranco Ferré, who was known as the

'architect of fashion.' After reading about him and discovering how architecture over the years has always influenced fashion, I started looking into architecture and found a lot of similarities as far as what it means to design and provide solutions for environments or bodies in the case of fashion. I then decided to major in architecture at UC Berkeley, because I felt that no matter what, it would make me a better designer overall. It would give me different perspectives and approaches to the way in which I design and I could use those tools forever. I believe architecture school gave me a more thoughtful approach to design. It was actually part of my plan.

The politics of meaning, representation and visual culture are central to your work. As an African designer in the diaspora, how have you distilled these vectors into your collections for the global market?

Our approach has always been about providing a message that many people around the world can relate to. Though I was born in Ghana, I grew up in California, so I have to tell a story that is true and authentic to me. For me, that

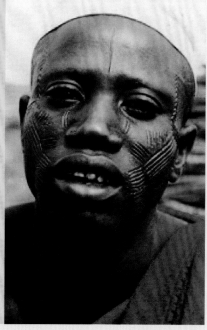

Opposite
Signature leather trapunto sheath dress by Mimi
Plange. Mimi Plange re-interprets scarification, a
visual culture found among people of disparate
cultures across Africa. The Italian trapunto
embroidery technique is applied to leather to mimic
the enigmatic yet resplendent art of scarification.

Above
The Trapunto embroidery bag from the scarification
collection. The bag is handcrafted from lambskin and
quilted in a custom scarification pattern.

story lies in having strong ties to my history and
culture, but also experiencing American culture
and finding a way to mould and mix those two
experiences together. We've always wanted to
pioneer a new thought about African fashion.
We do what is not expected. We discuss a
history and beauty of Africa that have not been
previously discussed. We are interested in
identity, and what it means to come from a
group or tribe, but still be an individual within
that group. We are interested in those who go
against the grain and formulate their own
identities, despite what society says he or she
should be. The stories we tell are subtle.
Visually, we want to make something the
consumer loves first, and that speaks to many
different cultures around the world. We weave
our culture and identity into the pieces that we
make by mimicking different forms of body
adornment, such as scarification, body
painting, piercings and other forms of
modification from the continent of Africa. We
are speaking to the beauty of the African body,
when the body itself, without textiles was used
as fashion. We are celebrating the African body
before colonization. We are celebrating ancient
rituals and African traditions by moving them
forward into today and beyond. We are mostly

tapping into an idea of an individual who wants distinction, who doesn't want to conform, and who believes in their own spirit and identity. This is an African spirit that is relatable to anyone.

Brand positioning is fundamental to luxury; however, positioning can be a costly venture. In what ways can brands with limited resources exploit storytelling as a tool for effective positioning?

As designers, we provide a service for people. For this reason, the greatest brands are the ones that people can identify with, be it because of the brand's core values or aesthetics. It is imperative, therefore, that storytelling transcends our individuality to encompass that which is true and resonates with your consumer. I think a great approach is to look at it as, 'this is not my story, it's our story'. In the early days of your business, if resources are limited, you can spend those days ironing out who your customer is and how to fulfil their needs with your product. It is important to create a valuable product before creating a story to sell it. Social media is an invaluable tool by which you curate your story to determine what works and what doesn't for your brand. As you crystallize your vision on social media, you will attract attention and opportunities to grow your business. As a start-up brand you must multi-task and can only accomplish much if you set goals and meet them.

When an opportunity avails to work with a celebrity or an established brand, think it through if the partnership will ultimately benefit your brand and resonate with your consumers. Positioning is about how you are presenting yourself to the world, and as a luxury brand you must channel the right visual impression. Focus is also critical to effective positioning, as your brand will be distinguished from the many if it exhibits proficiency or excellence in one specific product segment before diversifying. Focus also helps to fine tune your story into a clearer and more cohesive one over time. This isn't a race; it's a long journey.

Asymmetrical mustard wool blend blazer with silk organza shorts, paired with the Lebron XVIII Low X Mimi Plange sneakers. The Higher Learning collection is a celebration of School and Sport. It reflects the very first sneaker collaboration between LeBron James, Nike and Mimi Plange.

The conglomeration of luxury persists as the most potent threat to the success and sustenance of independent luxury brands. Do independent brands from marginalized regions such as Africa stand a chance in the global luxury industry?

Independent brands from Africa most definitely stand a chance in the global luxury industry, but not if their approach or goal is to be just like the luxury brands that already exist. Being a luxury brand is about having your own identity and being able to serve your consumers and keep them excited about your products, season after season. It's not about price or exclusivity – that's what it used to be about. Being a great designer is about learning from the past, but looking towards the future, without forgetting about the world right now. Who exactly is our customer, and where is she/he going when she wears our clothes? How can we tap into this new world? What solution can we provide our customers? You don't have to lose who you are, or your sense of self, but ultimately, this is a business, and it's not just about design. Design will get you noticed, but then, how will you actually run your business? If we can formulate compelling stories that resonate, there is no stopping independent designers from Africa. It's about identifying what makes the fashion on the continent so great, and then building a great story to allow you to share it. People just don't buy what is beautiful, they buy what they believe in. They can only believe in your vision, if you do.

What must designers of African origin do differently to establish a foothold in the global luxury economy?

I think there are many roads to success. There isn't just one way of doing something. Africa has some of the youngest and fastest-growing nations in the world. There are so many resources and opportunities there. Africa is already the birthplace of couture. There is no reason to seek that anywhere else. Embroidery, beading and all types of artisanal work are the foundation of African design. But design has to start with the people. The real way to establish a foothold is to solve a problem with your fashion. What's missing in the market? How can you make someone's life easier? How can you differentiate your brand? You have to be different in order to exist in the fashion arena. Forget about the old 'houses' and what worked in the past. Your path will be entirely different, you may not have even seen a path that looks like yours before because no one has done it your way. Be open to new ways of doing business in the world we live in right now. Being a designer is in so many ways being a researcher of people, their trends and their moods. Look beyond what is happening in the fashion industry and look to the actual people. You are trying to connect to the people through the fashion industry. The fashion industry is a tool in order to get to the people, but there are other ways to make connections, so if it doesn't happen that way, all is not lost. If you are in the diaspora, you have an ability to explore design through two lenses and that is a gift. Never forget that you are providing a service to your consumers, that is the only way to grow.

Tongoro Studio

Launched in 2016, Sarah Diouf's Tongoro Studio has etched its quintessential bold and playful aesthetics in the collective memory of the global luxury economy. Since its inception, the Senegal-based brand has shot to incredible heights, wooing the likes of models Naomi Campbell and Iman, and singers Alicia Keys, Kelly Rowland, Beyoncé and Burna Boy. *Tongoro* is the Sango (Central African language) word for star. Tongoro Studio experiments with bold prints and yet simple, billowing and refreshing silhouettes, offering a range of womenswear, menswear and accessories. In 2020, the brand launched a line of home products as part of its organic progression towards becoming a distinctive lifestyle brand. Harnessing the expertise from her previous roles in PR and communication, designer Sarah Diouf wears many hats, playing additional roles as a stylist, photographer, and editor of a digital magazine

Made (launched in 2021). She launched the 'Made in Africa' Campaign in 2021, a short documentary of the brand's wholly indigenous production chain. The thirty-minute documentary ushers the viewer along eclectic scenes on the streets of Dakar as the brand demonstrates its work with local craftsmen and communities in Senegal. 'Made in Africa' affirms Africa's potential and the possibilities amid the many challenges, while asserting that a globally relevant brand can be built with consideration for indigenous traditions and the environment.

Opposite
Cotton shirt from the menswear range Mogo and Zebra-inspired print jumpsuit from the Mbegell Collection by Tongoro Studio. Tongoro Studio creates simple silhouettes using bold prints inspired by culture, nature and the rhythm of Dakar's bustling lifestyle. The pieces drape elegantly and have become the go-to choice for outdoor wear and vacations.

What led to the establishment of Tongoro Studio?

In about 2015, when I began observing the African creative economy and noticed a rise of African brands and a surging interest in African fashion, it struck me that this was an industry at a tipping point. I also observed the attitude of European media to African brands, most of whom would only entertain African stories if they were told by major luxury companies. On the other side, budding African designers were positioning themselves to compete, especially in price points, with these established European brands. Tongoro was born out of a desire to bridge the disconnect, by providing accessibly priced luxury goods conveyed with authentic and compelling stories.

What is African luxury?

Luxury is subjective and, given the economic and socio-cultural context of Africa, it is imperative to approach in circumspect. I set out with a clear understanding of what luxury meant to me as a person: it was not about price nor the global reach of a brand, but lay in the details of the tactile fabric, the value of traditional techniques and their cultural symbolism. In that regard, Africa is a treasure trove of stories, with a heritage deeply amenable to luxury. African luxury is also experienced, guilt-free, by patronizing producers with a transparent and sustainable supply chain. I also believe that the limitations of African infrastructure, when it comes to mass production, compels us to master our crafts and to deliver excellence with so little, and this is where our luxury lies as a continent.

Left
Linen shirt from the menswear range Mogo by Tongoro Studio. Mogo translates the Tongoro spirit and brand ethos to masculinity. The pieces from this range are equally made to appear easy and relaxed, experimenting with fabrics such as polyester, linen and cotton.

Opposite
The Kata Jumpsuit from the Mbegeel collection by Tongoro Studio. Polyester print corset and jumpsuit with front cut out and maxi bell sleeves.

What inspired the 'Made in Africa' campaign?

In the early days of the brand, I encountered strong resistance to price – this, I observed, was linked to the unfavourable perception about the quality of African products. On the one hand, I felt it was unjust to compare our products with established international brands, which had an enduring heritage of excellence and the capital to invest in superior production infrastructure (more so when I understood the remarkable efforts African designers put into their work in the face of overwhelming challenges and infrastructure deficit). On the other hand, however, I saw this as a challenge to reframe the narrative of 'Made in Africa'. This quest informed my continued research into traditional production techniques, fabrics, prints and their meanings. The campaign explored the perpetual dialogue between mediums, craftsmanship, indigenous techniques and the communities at the heart of Africa's creative economy. Through the power of storytelling, 'Made in Africa' chronicled an integrated supply chain built on hard work and smart work, structure and consistency. However, beyond projecting Africa as a haven for excellence, 'Made in Africa' also spotlighted the beliefs and cultural values that underpin artforms both sacred and secular.

What unique contribution does Africa make to the global luxury economy?

I think sustainability is Africa's strength, and African brands must attend deliberately to their growth strategy in order not to repeat the mistakes of the global North. As a fledgling industry with no entrenched structures, it is imperative to build a robust supply chain on the continent with much consideration to the environment and the welfare of people within it.

What are your thoughts on the persistent appropriation of African culture?

I think brands can avoid the distasteful act of appropriation by involving the custodians of the specific cultures they are interested in exploiting for economic purposes, so they can also benefit from it. It is a way of showing respect. Unfortunately, for many brands, it is business as usual, and appropriation will persist so long as there are cultures to exploit, especially when the power imbalance between vulnerable cultures and predator brands remains. I think that the antidote is to tell our own stories through the power of social media.

Untitled piece from the MBEGEL campaign by Tongoro Studio. MBEGEL, which means love in Wolof inspired the pre-season campaign.

Glossary

Adinkra A collection of symbols with proverbial meanings, used in the production of fabrics, furniture and sacred artefacts among the Akan of Ghana.

Adire An indigo-dyed textile produced in southwestern Nigeria by Yoruba women, using organic plant dyes and a variety of resist-dyeing techniques.

Adire eleko A variant of the Adire cloth that employs stamping or hand painting for resist dyeing, resulting in fine resist details.

Adire oniko A variant of the Adire cloth that employs stitching or tying with raffia ropes, resulting in a spiral, irregular resist pattern.

Akan A meta-ethnicity spread along the central and coastal parts of present-day Ghana and Ivory Coast. The dominant Akan sub-groups include the Ashanti, Fante, Akyem, Bono, Agona, and Akwamu.

Akotifahana A handwoven textile composed of wild silk, weaver's banana and other indigenous fibres found in the highlands of Madagascar. It is woven by women from the Merino group and gained popularity in the nineteenth century.

Akwadan A garment by Juliana Norteye, also known as Chez Julie, adapting the toga style worn by men in parts of West Africa.

Akwete A handwoven textile that is associated with the Igbos domiciled in Akwete, a township in Abia State, Nigeria. It is woven from sisal-hemp fibres or raffia and incorporates geometric patterns for use as ceremonial cloth.

Alaari baba aso A handwoven and hand-embroidered textile used for hats and headwraps by the Yoruba of Nigeria.

Anziku The Anziku Kingdom, also known as the Tio Kingdom, is a precolonial Central African state found in the modern Republic of Congo. It was inhabited by the Teke people.

Asafo A regiment of highly skilled warriors, predominantly of the Fante people dotted along the coast of Ghana. The word is derived from sa (war) and fo (people).

Ashanti A sub-group of the Akan meta-ethnic group. The Ashanti people are located in middle belt of Ghana and are popular for their military prowess in precolonial Africa. The Ashanti Kingdom was known also for its mineral wealth and rich cultural heritage, and remains a powerful political and economic state in present-day Ghana.

Aso-Oke Literally translated as 'top cloth' aso-oke is a handwoven textile of the highest prestige. It is produced by the Yoruba of Nigeria but is widely adopted by the elite in West Africa and the global African diaspora.

Bamana/ Bambara The Bamana is the predominant tribe of the Bamana or Bambara Empire that occupied a part of present-day Mali.

Batakari A traditional smock worn predominantly in Northern Ghana and the Sahel belt of Africa. Also known as a fugu, it is made from strips of handwoven cloth and composed of indigenous cotton.

Batik A popular African textile made with wax resist and dyeing technique. The resist patterns are made using stamps created from wood or high-density foam boards. The fragile wax resist dyeing creates a uniform pattern with crackled effect.

Bogolanfini/ Bogolan An indigenous textile of Mali produced using mud and a process of natural oxidation. It involves dyeing locally woven cotton with a special dye bath and hand painting symbolic motifs before a final discharge with soap or bleach. The process results in a gradual transformation of the fabric into beautiful earthly hues.

Boubou A billowy and floor-length tunic with wide sleeves, often embellished with embroidery and worn by men and women in West Africa. It is traditionally made with cotton, wool, linen and silk.

Brocade A lustrous textile, usually made from satin or twill that is interwoven with motifs to create an intricate embroidery effect. It is made with a draw loom and was an item of trade and diplomacy in precolonial Africa, coming to the continent from Asia and the Levant.

Burqa A long and loose garment that conceals the body of women from head to toe, mostly allowing a slit around the eye area for visibility. Burqa is an important code of Islamic modesty.

Chiffon A lightweight and uniformly plain-woven sheer fabric used in making dresses.

Chintz A printed multi-coloured cotton fabric with a glazed finish and used predominantly for curtains and upholstery.

Coptic The Coptic Orthodox Church is a Christian Church with members in Egypt and Ethiopia.

Damask A heavy silk or linen fabric embellished with intricate, usually floral patterns that is interwoven for a rich visual and tactile effect.

Dinka A Nilotic ethnic group native to South Sudan. The Dinka are known for being tall and custodians to rich and resilient cultures.

Dipo A customary initiation rite and festival of the people of Krobo in the East of Ghana.

Dogon The Dogon are an ethnic group indigenous to the central plateau region of Mali, in West Africa, south of the Niger bend, near the city of Bandiagara, and in Burkina Faso.

Edo Natives of Benin City, the heartland of the ancient Benin Kingdom. Benin City is the capital of Edo State, a Federal State located Southern Nigeria.

Fugu See **Batakari**

Fulani A meta-ethnic group in Africa found in the Sahel and West Africa, but also spread widely across the North and Central parts of Africa.

Girken Zazzau A voluminous tunic made from handwoven indigenous cotton and embellished with embroidery. It originates from Kasar Zazzau in Northern Nigeria, an important axis in the network of textile trade in Northern Nigeria. It was the regalia of the elite and featured prominently at stately and ceremonial events.

Gonja Ethnic group found in the Savannah region of Ghana. The Gonja have been influenced by the Akan, Mande and Hausa people and are mainly Muslim.

Hausa An ethnic group found in north-western Nigeria and Southern Niger, the Hausa contain the Fulani, a large nomadic group found across Western and Central Africa.

Igbo A major ethnic group found predominantly in southeastern Nigeria.

Ikaki A prestigious variant of the Akwete cloth, handwoven to mimic the patterns on the tortoise shell.

Kaba A three-piece ensemble composed of a blouse, skirt and a waist wrapper worn by women in West Africa. The kaba, a corruption of the word 'cover', is inspired by the concealing uniforms of missionaries who advocated modesty.

Kente A vibrant and lustrous handwoven textile indigenous to the Ashanti and Ewe people of Ghana. Kente was woven originally from unravelled silk yarns but is now from rayon. Kente cloth is composed of woven strips sewn together.

Kentehene An official, usually a prominent, kente weaver, who is appointed by the Paramount Chief of the Ashanti Kingdom to preside over production and quality.

Khasa A high-quality variety of calico cloth that was manufactured and used for clothing in Mughal Empire in modern day Afghanistan.

Kimono A T-shaped garment with square sleeves indigenous to the Japanese.

Krobo An ethnic group located in the Eastern Region of Ghana, they are grouped as part of the Ga-Adangbe ethnolinguistic group and are the largest of the seven Ga-Adangbe groups.

Kuba People of the ancient Kuba Kingdom located presently in the Democratic Republic of Congo. The Kuba people are known for their beautiful handwoven and embroidered raffia Kuba/ Shoowa cloth.

Luxe Ubuntu A term coined to classify a luxury offering founded on African principles and ethics.

Mande A group of indigenous people found in West Africa. Mande may also refer to the language spoken by the people of the same ethnic group.

Manjak A handwoven textile produced by the Manjak people in West Africa. It sports vibrant colours and intricate geometric patterns similar to the kente.

Maasai The Maasai are a Nilotic ethnic group found in the northern, central and southern parts of Kenya and Tanzania. The Maasai are popular for their distinctive costume and jewellery customs.

Ndebele The Ndebele are a Nguni ethnic group native to Southern Africa. The Ndebele comprise two groups, the Nzunza and the Manala, each with their own distinct characteristics and dialects. The Ndebele are found mainly in the provinces of Mpumalanga, Gauteng and Limpopo. They are known for their bold wall decorations and geometrically designed beadwork.

Ndop Fabric made of strips of woven indigenous cotton and natural indigo dyes. Originally associated with funeral ceremonies and traditional rites among the Bamileke of Cameroon. The ethereal blue hues represent the sky, rain and powerful spirits.

Ngoni An ethnic group found in the Southern African countries of Malawi, Mozambique, Tanzania, Zimbabwe and Zambia. The Ngoni descend from the Nguni and Zulu people of KwaZulu-Natal in South Africa.

Oba The traditional ruler and custodian of the culture of the Edo people. The Edo are found predominantly in the Edo State of Southern Nigeria.

Okada A motorcycle improvised to serve as a commuter taxi, it is common in Nigeria and other African countries.

Organza A lightweight, sheer, plain woven fabric, originally made from silk.

Peuhl See **Fulani**

Plastex A proprietary material made from recycled plastic waste. It is used in manufacturing tote bags, purses and a variety of clothing and accessories.

Retso A printed, crimson-red textile common in Zimbabwe and traditionally associated with the invocation of ancestral spirits and the gods. Despite being popularized in contemporary fashion, it still maintains its mystique and dread.

Sangoma A traditional healer, diviner or priest of the Bantu people in South Africa.

Sanyan A prestigious variant of the aso-oke, woven with silk obtained from the cocoons of the Anaphe moth. It is dye-resistant and maintains an original ivory colour.

Sapeur or La Sape is a sub-culture of sharply dressed gentlemen and women found in Kinshasa and Brazzaville in the Democratic Republic of the Congo and Republic of Congo.

Shoowa See **Kuba**, the Shoowa are a small tribe from the Kingdom of Kuba.

Signare A group of wealthy women of African and French ancestry who became popular for their ostentatious lifestyles and distinctive taste in fashion and jewellery.

Sotho The Sotho-Tswana people inhabit the central plateau of Southern Africa, more specifically Botswana, Lesotho and northern parts of South Africa. They are distinguished from other Nguni tribes by their language and their belief in totems.

Sumanbrafo A composition of two words Suman and Brafo, Suman refers to an object used in the practice of magic, which over time assumes the status of a god. Brafo is a male warrior or executioner, usually of the royal guard. Sumanbrafo is hence loosely translated as the priest or servant of a Suman (god).

Taffeta A crisp, smooth and plain-woven fabric made from silk or rayon as well as acetate and polyester.

Trapunto A decorative, quilted design that produces a high relief using at least two layers of cloth by outlining the design in running stitch and padding if from the underside.

Tsonga The Tsonga people are of the Bantu ethnic group, and are found primarily in South Africa, Zimbabwe, Mozambique and Eswatini.

Tuareg The Tuareg are Berber-speaking pastoralists who inhabit parts of North and West Africa, including Libya, Mali, northern Nigeria, Fezzan and Algeria.

Xhosa A Nguni ethnic group in Southern Africa who hail originally from the Eastern Cape.

Yar Madaka A voluminous gown embellished with intricate handwoven and machine embroidery. The favourite ceremonial garment of traditional leaders, including Emirs and king makers in northern Nigeria.

Yoruba One of the principal languages of Nigeria spoken by the people of Igala, Edo, and Igbo. The Yoruba or Yoruba-speaking people are found predominantly in Nigeria, Benin and Togo.

Zazzau Also known as the Zaria Emirate, is a traditional state with headquarters in the city of Zaria located in Kaduna State, Nigeria. Zazzau was a prominent indigenous textile manufacturing hub in precolonial Africa.

Zulu The Zulu are a Nguni-speaking people found predominantly in KwaZulu-Natal province, South Africa. They belong to the Bantu meta-ethnic group and have close linguistic and cultural ties with the Swati and Xhosa. The Zulu are the single largest ethnic group in South Africa.

Endnotes

Chapter 1

1 Rovine V.L. (2009) *Viewing Africa through Fashion, Fashion Theory,* 13:2, 133-139.
2 Shumway R. (2014*) The Fante and the Transatlantic Slave Trade.* University of Rochester Press.
3 Rovine V.L. (2015) *African Fashion, Global Styles: Histories, Innovations, and Ideas You Can Wear.* Indiana University Press.
4 Wimmler J. (2017) *The Sun King's Atlantic: Drugs, Demons and Dyestuffs in the Atlantic World, 1640–1730.* Brill.
5 Loughran, K. (2015) *The Idea of Africa in European High Fashion: Global Dialogues, Fashion Theory,* 13:2, 243-271
6 Fee, S. (2013). *The Shape of Fashion: The Historic Silk Brocades* (akotifahana) of Highland Madagascar. African Arts. 46:3, 26-39.
7 Crabtree, C., and Stallebrass, P. (2002), *Beadwork: A World Guide.* Thames & Hudson.

Chapter 2

8 Rovine V.L. (2015).
9 Chris Seydou (1993) Interview with Rovine, Victoria. 6 March 1993. Published in Rovine, V.L. (2001) *Bogolan: Shaping Culture Through Cloth in Contemporary Mali.* Washington D.C. Smithsonian Institution Press.
10 Iqani, M. and Dosekun, S. (2019) Introduction in Iqani, M. and Dosekun, S. (eds). *African Luxury: Aesthetics and Politics.* Intellect Books.
11 Sicard, Marie-Claude, S. (2013) *Luxury Lies and Marketing: Shattering the Illusion of the Luxury Brand.* Palgrave Macmillan.
12 Statista (2018) 'Largest Luxury Markets in Africa as of 2018 by Revenue'. 13Euromonitor (2019). 'Luxury Goods in South Africa'.
14 PwC (2016) 'Prospects in the Retail and Consumer Goods in Ten Sub-Saharan African Countries'.
15 Martin-Leke S., Ellis E. (2014) T*owards a Definition of Authentic African Luxury: Luxe Ubuntu.* In: Atwal G., Bryson D. (eds) *Luxury Brands in Emerging Markets.* Palgrave Macmillan.
16 Beckwith, N., Bettelheim, J., Cozier, C., Mapily, J.J., and Recker, K. (2010) in Sims, L.S. and King-Hammond, L. *The Global Africa Project.* Prestel.
17 Adler, P. Barnard, N. (1992) *African Majesty*: The Textile Art of the Ashanti and Ewe. Thames & Hudson.
18 Strong, C. (1997). The Problems of Translating Fair Trade Principles into Consumer Purchase Behaviour. *Marketing Intelligence and Planning,* 15(1), 32-37.

Bibliography

Adler, P. and Barnard, N. *African Majesty: The Textile Art of the Ashanti and Ewe.* Thames and Hudson, 1992
Atmore, A. and Stacey, G. Black Kingdoms, *Black Peoples: The West African Heritage.* Harper Collins. 1985.
Atwal, G. & Bryson, D. *Luxury Brands in Emerging Markets,* Palgrave Macmillan, 2014.
Helen, J. *New African Fashion.* Prestel, 2011.
Campbell, D., Rey, C., Ehmann, S & Klanten, R. (eds). *The Craft and the Makers: Tradition with Attitude.* Gestalten. 2014.
Crabtree, C. & Stallebrass, P. *Beadwork: A World Guide.* Rizzoli, 2002.
Drewal, J. & Schildkrout, E. *Dynasty and Divinity: Ife Art in Ancient Nigeria.* Museum for African Art and Fundación Marcelino Botín. 2009.
Eicher, J. B & Ross, D. H. (eds). *Encyclopedia of World Dress and Fashion: Africa.* Oxford University Press. 2010.
Gillow, J. *African Textiles: Color and Creativity Across a Continent.* Thames and Hudson. 2016.
Gott, S. and Loughran, K. (eds). *Contemporary African Fashion,* Indiana University Press. 2010.
Fisher, A. *Africa Adorned,* Harry N. Abrams. 1984.
Kriger, C.E. *Cloth in West African History.* Altamira Press. 2006.
Marie-Claude, S. *Luxury, Lies and Marketing: Shattering the Illusion of the Luxury Brand.* Palgrave Macmillan. 2013.
Marie-Louise, L. *Beads of Life: Eastern and Southern African Beadwork from Canadian Collections.* Canadian Museum of Civilization. 2005.
McNaughton, P.R. *The Mande Blacksmiths: Knowledge, Power, and Art in West Africa.* Indiana University Press. 1993.
McNeil, P. & Riello, G. *Luxury, A Rich History.* Oxford University Press. 2016.
Musée Dapper. *Ghana Yesterday and Today.* Editions Dapper. 2003.
Ricca, M. & Robins, R. *Meta-Luxury: Brands and the Culture of Excellence.* Palgrave Macmillan. 2012.
Rovine, V.L. African Fashion, *Global Style: Histories, Innovations, and Ideas You Can Wear.* Indiana University Press. 2015.
Shumway, R. *The Fante and the Transatlantic Slave Trade.* University of Rochester Press. 2011.
Sims, L. S. & King-Hammond, L. *The Global Africa Project.* Prestel. 2010.
Sparks, R.J. *Where the Negroes Are Masters: An African Port in the Era of the Slave Trade.* Harvard University Press. 2014.
Thomas, D. *Deluxe: How Luxury Lost Its Lustre.* Penguin Books. 2007.
Wimmler, J. *The Sun King's Atlantic: Drugs, Demons and Dyestuffs in the Atlantic World,* 1640-1730. Brill. 2017.

Index

Page numbers in *italics* indicate
illustration captions.

Photo credits

Grateful acknowledgement is extended for the use of the following images. Every effort has been made to trace all copyright holders. The publisher apologizes for any unintentional error and will be pleased to insert the appropriate acknowledgement in any subsequent edition.

Front cover: Courtesy Jiamini, Photo: Kadara Enyeasi, Model: Zainab Alade, Represented by 90s Models Management, Nigeria, Make-up: Obidike Uchechukwu, Producer: A Whitespace Creative Agency, Produced with support from Ethical Fashion Initiative and EU International partnerships; Back cover: Courtesy Johanna Bramble, Photo: Johanna Bramble; p6 Courtesy Deola Sagoe, Photo: TY Bello; p8 Courtesy Duaba Serwa, Photo: Josh Sisly, Model: Sadia AJ, Stylist: Kojo Africa, Make-up: Loox Artistry; p10 Courtesy AAKS, Photo: Cara Johnson Photography; p15 Granger Historical Picture Archive/Alamy Stock Photo; p17 © Carol Beckwith and Angela Fisher; p19 Heritage Image Partnership Ltd/Alamy Stock Photo; p21 © Yaw Pare Photography; p22 © Carol Beckwith and Angela Fisher; p23 ullstein bild/Getty Images; p24 Per-Anders Pettersson/Getty Images; p25 © Sarah Errington/Eye Ubiquitous/Hutchison; p26 Chronicle/Alamy Stock Photo; p27 Echoes/Redferns/Getty Images; p28 © Yves Saint Laurent © All rights reserved; p30 Bibliothèque nationale de France, Paris; p31 RMN-Grand Palais /Dist. Photo SCALA, Florence; p33 © Carol Beckwith and Angela Fisher; p35 Michel Huet/Gamma-Rapho/Getty Images; p36t Dallas Museum of Art, anonymous gift, image courtesy Dallas Museum of Art; p36c Dallas Museum of Art, The Eugene and Margaret McDermott Art Fund, Inc., image courtesy Dallas Museum of Art; p36b Dallas Museum of Art, anonymous gift in honor of Professor Roy Sieber, image courtesy Dallas Museum of Art; p37t Dallas Museum of Art, anonymous gift, image courtesy Dallas Museum of Art; p37b Dallas Museum of Art, anonymous gift in honour of Professor Roy Sieber, image courtesy Dallas Museum of Art; p38 Dallas Museum of Art, African Collection Fund, image courtesy Dallas Museum of Art; p39 Bennett Raglin/Getty Images; p40t, c & b Photo © The Trustees of the British Museum. All rights reserved; p42t & b Photo © The Trustees of the British Museum. All rights reserved; p42c Metropolitan Museum of Art, Gift of Dr. and Mrs. Pascal James Imperato, 2015, Image copyright Metropolitan Museum of Art/Art Resource/Scala, Florence; p43 Michele Burgess/Alamy Stock Photo; p44l & r Photo © The Trustees of the British Museum. All rights reserved; p45 MyLoupe/Universal Images Group/Getty Images; p46 Photo © The Trustees of the British Museum. All rights reserved; p47 robertharding/Alamy Stock Photo; p48l Photo © The Trustees of the British Museum. All rights reserved; p48r Education Images/Universal Images Group/Getty Images; p49 Anton_Ivanov/Shutterstock; p50 Photo © François Goudier, reproduced with kind permission of Aboubakar Fofana; p51 Reuters/Alamy Stock Photo; p52 Album/Alamy Stock Photo; pp53 & 54 © Carol Beckwith and Angela Fisher; p55l National Museum of African Art, Smithsonian Institution, Washington, D.C., Gift of Dr. Marian Ashby Johnson; p55r The New York Public Library; p57t Travelpix/Alamy Stock Photo; p57bl & br © Carol Beckwith and Angela Fisher; p58 Margaret Courtney-Clarke/Africa Media Online; p63 Photo: Akin

Adegunju AEC Studios, Models: Chioma, Nkem, Cherem, Stylist: Teni Sagoe, Atinudah Concepts, Make up: Juliet Onwubiko, Ebon Beauty, Head Pieces: SS21 Ghen Ghen Collection; 64 Courtesy Shade Thomas-Fahm; p65 Photo courtesy Samuel P. Harn Museum of Art, University of Florida,Gainesville; Gift of Edith François, reproduced with permission from the Estate of Chez Julie, The Estate of Chez Julie represented by Fashion Forum Africa; p66l Seyllou/AFP/GettyImages; p66r Photo courtesy Nabil Zorkot; p68 Olympia de Maismont/Anadolu Agency/Getty Images; p69 Issouf Sanogo/AFP/Getty Images; p70 Andreas Solaro/AFP/Getty Images; p73 Nic Bothma/EPA/Shutterstock; p74 Courtesy The Lotte Accra, Photo: Josh Sisly; p75 Emmanuel Arewa/AFP/Getty Images; p77 Fadel Senna/AFP/Getty Images; p78 Etienne Tordoir/WireImage/Getty Images; p79 Sunday Alamba/AP/Shutterstock; p80 Oupa Bopape/Gallo Images/Getty Images; p82t Album/Alamy Stock Photo; p82b Marvel/Disney/Kobal/Shutterstock; p83t AFP/Getty Images; p83b Amazon Studios/Moviestore/Shutterstock; p84 Dominique Charriau/WireImage/Getty Images; p85t Ovidiu Hrubaru/Alamy Stock Photo; p85bl Bebeto Matthews/AP/Shutterstock; p85br Ian Langsdon/EPA-EFE/Shutterstock; p86 Andy Kropa/Getty Images; p89 Christie Brown, Photo: Phloshop; p90 Courtesy AAKS; p91 Courtesy Reform Studio; p93 Photo: Kadara Enyeasi, Model: Zainab Alade, Represented by 90s Models Management, Nigeria, Make-up: Obidike Uchechukwu, Producer: A Whitespace Creative Agency, Produced with support from Ethical Fashion Initiative and EU International partnerships; p96 Courtesy MmusoMaxwell, Photo: Tatenda Chidora, Models: Connie @ ICE Models JHB & Desiree (RSA) Stylist & Art Direction: Chloe Andrea, Make-up & Hair: Bassie Seripe, Production: Lampost Production - Carlien De Kock ; p98 Courtesy Adama Paris, Photo: Bilal Moussa; p99 Courtesy Kapoeta by Ambica, Photo: Sunny Dolat, Model: Juliet Kiruhij: Make-up: Sinitta Akello; p100 Courtesy I.AM.ISIGO, Creative Direction: Bubu Ogisi, Photo: Chris Okoigun, Model: Adejoke Adesope; p101 Courtesy Reform Studio; p102 Courtesy MmusoMaxwell, Photo: everydaypeoplestories, Model: Kubie Makobo, Fashion Director: Thobeka Maduna Mbane, Make-up: Tammimbambo; p103 Allëdjo Studio, Creative Director & Photo: Kassim Lassissi; p104 Courtesy Pistis, Photo: Phloshop, Model: suma_elle, Make-up: Valerie Lawson & CVL Beauty, Hair: Revup Salon; p105 Courtesy Zashadu, Medina Dugger, Sophia Kahlenberg, Israel Aigbederon; p106 Courtesy Christie Brown, Photo: Duque Photography; p107 Courtesy AAKS, Photo: Cara Johnson Photography; p108 Courtesy John Tchoudi, Sika'a; p109 Courtesy Jiamini, Photo: Kadara Enyeasi, Model: Zainab Alade, Represented by 90s Models Management, Nigeria, Make-up: Obidike Uchechukwu, Producer: A Whitespace Creative Agency, Produced with support from Ethical Fashion Initiative and EU International partnerships; pp110-11 Courtesy David Tlale, Models: Kore Thando, sedi22000 & Dylan Wentzel, Hair: Sonnymagic, Make-up: Bjornakabee, Styling: Betty Becker and Sahil Harilal; p112 Courtesy Pichulik, Photo: Michael Oliver; p113 Courtesy Simon and Mary, Agency: Jana + Koos, Photo: Travys Owen, Model: Shakes Fatman, Stylist: Gabrielle Kannemeyer, Make-up: Suaad Jeppie, Hair:

Suaad Jeppie; p114 Courtesy Lukhanyo Mdingi, Photo: Mousa Sow; p115 Courtesy Lukhanyo Mdingi, Photographer: Luke Houba, Model: Pivot @ 20 Models, Make-up: Inga Hewett, Stylist's Assistant: Keenan Martin; p116tl & tr Courtesy Lukhanyo Mdingi, Photo: Jarred Figgins, Models: Roldy and Pivot @ 20 Models, Stylist: Lukhanyo Mdingi, Make-up & Hair: Justine Nomz; p116bl & br Courtesy Lukhanyo Mdingi, Photo: Jarred Figgins, Model: Geena @ Topco, Stylist, Lukhanyo Mdingi, Make-up & Hair: Justine Nomz; p119t Courtesy Lukhanyo Mdingi, Photo: Jarred Figgins, Models: Roldy and Pivot @ 20 Models, Stylist: Lukhanyo Mdingi, Make-up & Hair: Justine Nomz; p119b Courtesy Lukhanyo Mdingi, Photo: Jarred Figgins, Model: Geena @ Topco, Stylist: Lukhanyo Mdingi, Make-up & Hair: Justine Nomz; pp120-125 Courtesy Adele Dejak; p126 Courtesy Thebe Magugu, Photo: Aart Verrips, Model: Thebe Magugu, Stylist: Chloe-Andrea Welgemoed, Make-up: Annice Roux Gerber, Hair: Saadique Ryklief; p127 Courtesy Thebe Magugu, Photo: Aart Verrips, Model: Anyon Asola, Stylist: Thebe Magugu, Make-up: Orlioh; p129t Courtesy Thebe Magugu, Photo: Kristin Lee Moolman, Model: Catherine - Fab Models, Stylist: Chloe – Andrea Welgemoed, Make-up: Alexander J Botha, Hair: Khomotšo Moloto & Saadique Ryklief; p129b Courtesy Thebe Magugu, Photo: Aart Verrips, Model: Don Makon, Stylist: Chloe – Andrea Welgemoed, Make-up: Annice Roux Gerber, Hair: Saadique Ryklief; pp130 & 131 Courtesy Thebe Magugu, Photo: Travys Owen, Model: Vanessa Ngolo, Stylist: Thebe Magugu, Make-up: Orlioh, Hair: Ntombomzi Lekgoro; p132 Courtesy Kat van Duinen, Photo: Claire Nicola, Stylist: Kat van Duinen; p133 Courtesy Kat van Duinen, Photo: Diaan de Beer, Model: Andrea Lucrezia Perreca – Fusion Models, Stylist: Kat van Duinen, Make-up & Hair: Natasha Papadopoulos; p134 Courtesy Kat van Duinen, Photo: Jacobus Snyman, Stylist: Lyal Seba; p135 Courtesy Kat van Duinen, Photo: Diaan de Beer, Model: Alex – Fusion Models, Stylist: Kat van Duinen, Make-up & Hair: Alet Viljoen; p137 Courtesy Kat van Duinen, Photo: Gavin Goodman, Model: Zana & Aude – Boss Models, Lebo – Ice Genetics, Stylist: Bev Nates, Make-up & Hair: Raine Tauber; p138 Courtesy Peuhl Vagabond, Photo: Fredo H., Model & Stylist: Dyenaa Diaw, Make-up & Hair: Makeupbiuty; p139 Courtesy Peuhl Vagabond, Photo: Viana Photography, Model: Koudedia Sora, Stylist: Peuhl Vagabond/Diby Magassa, Make-up: Sarama Makeup, Hair: Kaamila Hair; p140 Courtesy Peuhl Vagabond, Photo: Ian Hippolyte, Model: Kamara Djily, Stylist: Peuhl Vagabond, Make-up: Ruben Mas, Hair: Fab Hair; p142 Courtesy Peuhl Vagabond, Photo: Fredo H., Model: Daouda, Stylist: Peuhl Vagabond, Make-up: Adam's Make-up, Hair: Fab Hair; p143 Courtesy Peuhl Vagabond, Photo: Fredo H., Model: Ando, Stylist: Peuhl Vagabond, Make-up: Adam's Make-up, Hair: Dyenaa Diaw; p144 Courtesy Tokyo James; pp145 & 146l & r Courtesy Tokyo James; p147 Courtesy Tokyo James, Photo: Mikey Oshai, Stylist: Dalia Fardoun / Baba Tunde Oyeyemi; p148 Courtesy Tokyo James, Photo: Akin Adegunju, Stylist: Tokyo James; p150 Courtesy Maison ARTC, Photo: Suzane Holtgrave; pp151, 152, 153 & 154 Courtesy Maison ARTC, Photo: Artsi Ifrah, model: Tilila; p156 Courtesy Imane Ayissi, Photo: Stéphane de Bourgies; p157 Courtesy Imane Ayissi, Photo: Fabrice Malard, Model:

Bintouka, Make-up: Militina, Hair: Manon Cana Skovienova, Special acknowledgement: Foundryftlab and Haute Couture Week; p158 Courtesy Imane Ayissi, Photo: Fabrice Malard, Model: Hedvig Maigre, Make-up: Militina, Hair: Manon Cana Skovienova, Special acknowledgement: Foundryftlab and Haute Couture Week; p160l Courtesy Imane Ayissi, Photo: Fabrice Malard, Model: Coumbelle Kane, Make-up: Anne-Esther & Dina Ebimbe, Manon Cana Skovienova, Lena Autusse/Magali Guitter, Special acknowledgement: Mephistopheles Production, Hotel Le Marois, Area Box; p160r Courtesy Imane Ayissi, Photo: Fabrice Malard, Model: Hedvig Maigre, Make-up: Anne-Esther & Dina Ebimbe, Manon Cana Skovienova, Lena Autusse/Magali Guitter, Special acknowledgement: Mephistopheles Production, Hotel Le Marois, Area Box; p161l Courtesy Imane Ayissi, Photo: Fabrice Malard, Model: Joony Kim, Make-up: Anne-Esther & Dina Ebimbe, Manon Cana Skovienova, Lena Autusse/Magali Guitter, Special acknowledgement: Mephistopheles Production, Hotel Le Marois, Area Box; p161r Courtesy Imane Ayissi, Photo: Fabrice Malard, Model: Laurie Orsini, Make-up: Anne-Esther & Dina Ebimbe, Manon Cana Skovienova, Lena Autusse/ Magali Guitter, Special acknowledgement: Mephistopheles Production, Hotel Le Marois, Area Box; p162 Courtesy Taibo Bacar; p163 Courtesy Taibo Bacar, Photo: Dan Carter, Model: Elizma Esterhuyse, Make-up & Hair: Raela Bacar; p164 Courtesy Taibo Bacar, Photo: Dan Carter, Models: Papi & Kristina Liliana Nova, Make-up & Hair: Raela Bacar; p165 Courtesy Taibo Bacar, Photo: Dan Carter, Models: Papi & Elizma Esterhuyse, Make-up & Hair: Raela Bacar; p166 Courtesy Taibo Bacar, Photo: Dan Carter, Model: Kristina Liliana Nova, Make-up & Hair: Raela Bacar; p167 Courtesy Taibo Bacar, Photo: Bambino, Model: Jessica, Make-up & Hair: Raela Bacar; pp168 Courtesy Johanna Bramble Photo: Joana Choumali; pp169-70 Courtesy Johanna Bramble, Photo: Johanna Bramble, p,171 Courtesy Johanna Bramble, Photo: Johanna Bramble, Model Antoine Diedhiou; p. 172 Courtesy Johann Bramble, Photo: Johanna Bramble; pp174 Courtesy T-Michael p174t Courtesy T-Michael; p174b Courtesy T-Michael, Photo: Bent René Synnevåg, Model: Kalaf Angelo; p175 Courtesy T-Michael, Photo: Martin Hoye, Model: Youssou Diop, Stylist: T-Michael; p176 Courtesy T-Michael, Photo: Mamadee King Kabba, Model: Youssou Diop, Stylist: T-Michael, Set: Henrik Håkansson's '101 Tree Branches & Boughs at Tårnsalen Kode 4 Bergen; p177 Courtesy T-Michael, Photog: Bent René Synnevåg, Model: Sonja Wanda; p179l Courtesy T-Michael, Model: Paul Marcel Malemo, Stylist: T-Michael; p179r Courtesy T-Michael, Photographer: Dulce Daniel, Model: Simon Villaeys, Stylist: Tania Dioespirro; p180 Courtesy Mimi Plange, Photo: Emmanuel André; p181 Courtesy Mimi Plange, Photo: Note Peter George, Model: Jessica Millin, Stylist: Stacey Jones, Make-up: Joanne Gair, Hair: Linh Nguyen; pp182 & 183 Courtesy Mimi Plange; p184 Courtesy Mimi Plange, Photo: Lindsay Adler, Model: Somalia Knight, Stylist: Stacey Jones, Make-up: Joanne Gair, Hair: Linh Nguyen; p186 Courtesy Tongoro Studio, Photo: Bizenga Da Silvo; pp187-190 Courtesy Tongoro Studio, Photo: Sarah Diouf; p200 Courtesy Mastoor, Photo: Mounir Raji.

Acknowledgements

This book would have remained a concept in abstraction without the help of designers, photographers, editors, proofreaders, and a nucleus of supportive family and friends. My utmost gratitude goes to the designers who believed in this project and welcomed me into the inner sanctums of their design world. I can only say, bravo! The preservation and promotion of your legacy is the spirit of this volume.

Special thanks to the legendary Shade Thomas-Fahm for the hearty and thought-provoking conversation and couture Queen Deola Sagoe for penning a captivating foreword. Thank you to Sophie Wise, commissioning editor at LKP (now Quercus Books), for guiding the project to fruition, and to the relentless Sophie Hartley, picture researcher of the project.

I thank all the discerning voices that anchored me in accomplishing this noble feat. They include my legal advisor and business coach, Judith Aidoo-Saltus; Shaun Borstrock of the University of Hertfordshire; Veronica B. Manlow at Brooklyn College; Erica de Greef, director of African Fashion Research Institute (AFRIdigital) and curator at large for Fashion at Zeits MOCAA; Awo Abena Amoa Sarpong of the University of Cape Coast, whose library of out-of-print African art books kept me spellbound; Frederica Brooksworth of the Council for International African Fashion Education (CIAFE); Roberta Annan of AFF; Amukelani Muthambi of the University of Johannesburg; Polly Savage of SOAS University of London; Jessica Spencer; Vimbai Shire; Nana Addo-Gyampoh (Esq); Ps Justice Anderson; Fauzi Fahm, director of Shade Thomas-Fahm Legacy Project (STFLP); Lungi Morrison; and my sisters, Franklina Appiah-Nimo and Christina Appiah-Nimo.

Finally, my heartfelt gratitude to the illustrious list of authors, whose invaluable research and archival work underpin this volume.

Desert Caravan Collection SS22 by Mastoor. This collection is inspired by the scenery in the desert and carries the story of nomads and desert people living with natural resources.